the beatles · 365 days

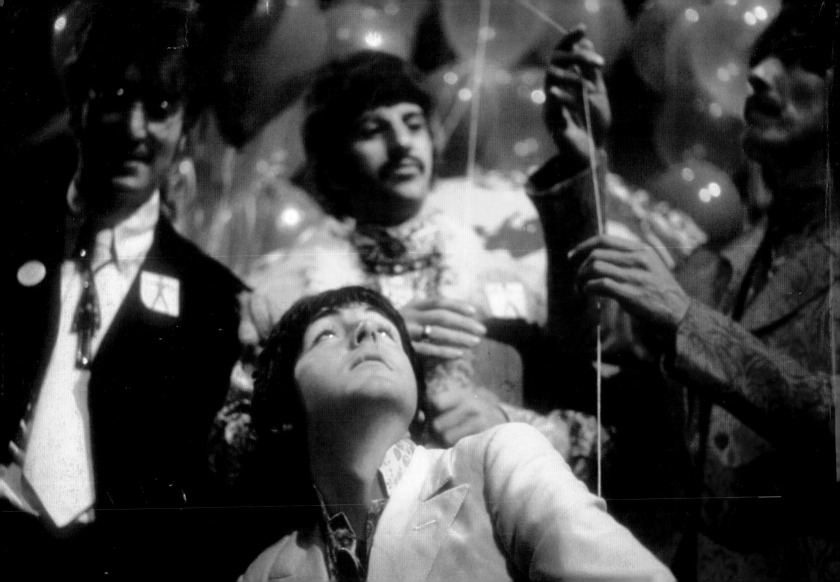

gettyimages· SIMON WELLS

the beatles · 365 days

HARRY N. ABRAMS, INC., PUBLISHERS

The Beatles: Introduction

Millions of words have been written about the Beatles, probably more than any other young men of the twentieth century, and yet the Beatles' enormous celebrity ensures that any new nugget of information is still considered news-worthy enough to make front-page headlines. Tales of the group's "rags to riches" success are now legendary and can be used as guideposts for seekers of similar fortune and fame. The footsteps they trod from Liverpool to London, Hamburg to New York, are now care-fully orchestrated tourist trails. The souls they left behind recount their asso-ciations with a certain wistfulness at having been left off the magical caravan.

As John Lennon so eloquently wrote, "Some are dead and some are living," and yet it is ironic that post-millennium only two of the group have lived to see sixty.

The Beatles were undoubtedly the most photographed men in the 1960s, but as one wades through the multitude of books that seem to emerge on a weekly basis, the images have a weary familiarity to them. It was a joy then for me to discover this archive of unique images, most of which have never been seen, at the Hulton-Getty collection in West London. Newspapers and maga-zines that covered the tumultuous rise of the group during the 1960s often shot much more than there was space to pub-lish. Somehow, these outtakes ended up in the basement at Hulton-Getty, and the best of these are now collected in this single volume. These photographs offer a new view of the greatest, most influential band to ever grace this planet, and as such, are priceless recol-lections of a magical time. The Beatles brightened our lives then and continue to do so today. Long may they shine and illuminate our darkest hours.

We hope you enjoy the show!

Simon Wells
Sussex, England
December 2004

(PAGE 2) The Beatles at the launch party for their single, "All You Need is Love." June 24, 1967.

(OPPOSITE) A RIGHT SOAKING During their first full day of filming *Help!*, the Beatles are in the swim-ming pool of the Nassau Beach Hotel while shooting some of the closing sequences. February 23, 1965.

From a Whisper to a Shout, 1963–1965

"The thing I'm afraid of is growing old. I hate that. You get old and you've missed it somehow. The old always resent the young and vice versa."
—*John Lennon*, 23
FROM WOOLTON, LIVERPOOL

"Don't say 'For Heaven's sake, say we're the new youth,' because that's a lot of old rubbish."
—*Paul McCartney*, 21
FROM ALLERTON, LIVERPOOL

"Naturally, I am part of my generation. I like the way people bring things out in the open. I'd hate it if when you spoke about sex everybody curled away."
—*George Harrison*, 20
FROM SPEKE, LIVERPOOL

"I'd like to end up sort of unforgettable."
—*Ringo Star*, 23
FROM DINGLE, LIVERPOOL

Where it all began. The Cavern, 10 Mathew Street, Liverpool, England. A dank, sweaty basement club that had formerly been used as a vegetable storage area. The Beatles played at the club 292 times before it finally closed in 1966. Some years later, with little regard for its historical significance, the venue was demolished to make way for a ventilation shaft to serve the city's underground system. Liverpool record shop proprietor Brian Epstein first saw the Beatles perform at the club on November 9, 1961.

Brian Epstein: "I was immediately struck by their music, their beat, and their sense of humor onstage. And even afterward when I met them, I was struck again by their personal charm. And it was there that really it all started . . ."

February 10, 1963

Four northern lads down south. Not yet
used to the subtlety of photo sessions,
the boys nonetheless oblige photogra‐
pher Cyrus Andrews as best they can by
sitting on a table in the lounge of the
Sloane Court Hotel in Chelsea, London.
The Beatles' recording and television
commitments required them to spend
more and more time in the capital, and
although they were all still living in
Liverpool, they were cautious about
moving to a more permanent base
in the metropolis.

Ringo: "I don't think any of us are
moving. We must have a base in London,
you know, because we're there more
than we are in Liverpool at the moment.
But we're not moving our houses."

February 17, 1963

LUCKY STARS

The momentum was gathering pace.
With a record deal secured with the
mighty EMI organization, and publish-
ing courtesy of Dick James, the Beatles
had the strongest base to launch their
assault on the musical summit of the
world. Their spot on the highly influential show *Thank Your Lucky Stars* may
have been the group's ninth television
appearance, but it was a rare network
exposure for the band and helped spread
the Beatles' message to the four corners
of the United Kingdom.

April 10, 1963

Working up a sweat at the Top Rank
Majestic Ballroom in Birkenhead,
Liverpool. After several months slicked
back, Ringo's mop had finally fallen into
the familiar Beatles' shape. The image
that was to be imitated throughout the
world was now complete.

George: "I don't think any of us had
been bothered with having haircuts,
and it was always long. Paul and John
went to Paris and came back with it—
something like this. And I went to the
baths and came out with it like this."

Rehearsals for the Beatles' first appearance on TV's *Sunday Night at the London Palladium* in the heart of London's West End. The program, ATV's flagship Sunday night entertainment show, was seen by more than 15 million viewers, and elevated the Beatles into the nation's consciousness as major stars. The scenes outside the London Palladium that evening took the press by surprise and led to banner headlines the next day, along with the coinage of the word "Beatlemania" (a term that has stuck to this day). Despite the brouhaha, the Beatles were still cautious of just how long their success might actually last.

John: "'How long are you going to last?' Well, you can't say, you know? You can be bigheaded and say, 'Yeah, we're going to last ten years.' But as soon as you've said that, you think, 'We're lucky if we last three months.'"

Paul: "We can't keep playing the same sort of music until we're about forty. Old men playing 'From Me to You'? Nobody is going to want to know at all about that sort of thing."

George: "Well, I suppose we'll stay doing this sort of stuff for a couple of years. Naturally we won't be able to stay at this level. But, we should have another two years at least, I think."

October 13, 1963

The Beatles and Bruce Forsyth
rehearse the traditional coda to *Sunday
Night at the London Palladium*. One
interesting factor of the Beatles' early
success was the ability of the group
(under manager Brain Epstein's savvy
and intuitive guidance) to embrace
every situation that arose. They even
agreed to prance around on a rotating
dais, confirming that the "Cheeky
Loveable Mop-tops" were willing to
give anything a try. Coincidentally, the
Rolling Stones later appeared on the
show, although they would cause a
minor uproar when they refused to
mount the spinning stage at the end
of the evening.

BOUND FOR SWEDEN

After a morning's recording at EMI studios for the group's forthcoming album, *With the Beatles*, the boys convened at London's Heathrow Airport for a trip to Sweden, their first engagement outside Britain since December 1962. The Scandinavian girls in the audience proved no less enthusiastic than their counterparts in the United Kingdom though, and several defied security to reach the stage and leap, literally, onto the group.

Paul: "It was a bit difficult playing with one on my back. Two girls jumped up onto the stage one night and one climbed on me and the other on George."

November 4, 1963

Grabbing a quick coffee after lunch at the Mapleton Hotel, adjacent to the Prince of Wales Theatre on London's Coventry Street. Here, the Beatles were rehearsing for their most prestigious performance to date, the 1963 *Royal Variety Performance*. Never was the Beatles' bond closer than it was in the early days of Beatlemania. Everything revolved around their equal involvement in their daily schedule, and as a result of spending so much time together a startling uniformity arose in their clothes and deportment.

John: "You know the way people begin to look exactly like their dogs? Well, we're beginning to look like each other."

November 4, 1963

MR. CONFIDENT

Of all the Beatles, it was Paul who most
heartily endorsed Brian Epstein's obsession with securing the patronage of the
higher echelons of British society and in
presenting the Beatles as the darlings of
that crowd. Their appearance on the
Royal Variety Show was confirmation of
their meteoric rise on every rung of
Britain's social ladder.

Q: "Paul, have you thought about your
act for this show yet? Any changes in
the act, or is it going to be, you know,
the usual routine?"

Paul: "No, we'll have to change it, I'm
sure. We can't do the same thing all the
time. We haven't thought about what
we're going to do yet."

November 4, 1963

Rehearsals at the *Royal Variety Show* with Marlene Dietrich and Tommy Steele. For weeks, the group had carefully rehearsed their patter for the *Royal Variety* performance, aware that it had to conform to the public perception of their cheeky, mop-top image. Paul was satisfied with his remark preceding the song "Till There Was You" that it had recently been recorded by their "favorite American group, Sophie Tucker" (a sly dig at her considerable size). John was gung ho about his rejoinder for the audience to "rattle their jewelry," although he would test manager Brian Epstein's tolerance by threatening to insert a few *f* words to liven up the stiffs in the audience.

John: "Will the people in the cheaper seats clap your hands? And the rest of you, if you'll just rattle your jewelry."

SLOUGH

It's all over and the boys line up for
the presentation to the Queen Mother.
Among other things, she asked the boys
where their next performance was to be.
Paul told her, "Slough." "Ah," she said,
visibly excited by the prospect. "That's
near us!" Although, publicly at least,
they were excited at the opportunity to
perform at the most prestigious event in
Theaterland's calendar, the Beatles
refused to appear on the show again.

John: "We were asked discreetly to do
it every year after that but we always
said, 'Stuff it!'"

Queuing for tickets at the Lewisham
Odeon for the group's two shows on
December 18. After the tumultuous
success of the *Royal Variety Show*, the
Beatles were now the nation's favorite
quartet, and scenes such as these in
South London were common all over
the country. Even psychologists were
being called upon to describe the phenomenon of Beatlemania. The ritualistic
pelting of the group with Jelly Beans
was leapt upon by the press as symboliz-
ing something deeper than it probably
was. (George had innocently remarked
that the group liked the taste of them.)

From the *News of the World*,
November 1963: "They are subcon-
sciously preparing for motherhood.
Their frenzied screams are a rehearsal
for that moment. Even the Jelly [Beans]
are symbolic."

(OPPOSITE TOP) THE EPSTEIN STABLE OF STARS
From left: The Beatles, Gerry and the
Pacemakers, Billy J. Kramer and the
Dakotas, and Brian Epstein line up for a
group photograph. Epstein's management
literally collected the cream of Merseyside
talent, and using the Beatles' fame as
collateral, ensured recording contracts
and attendant press coverage for his roster
of Liverpool entertainers.

The Observer: "Our correspondent
does not get from Mr. Epstein the
impression of a brilliant manipulator,
but of a shrewd young man who has
caught the lightning."

(OPPOSITE BOTTOM)
Outside of the Winter Gardens,
Bournemouth, it was a familiar scene,
with police lined up to ensure a safe
passage for both fans and Beatles alike.
It was reported that police authorities
across the country were having their
precious resources stretched to the limit
to staff the various Beatles events. A
more humorous side to the issue also
emerged—many of the constabularies
were competing against each other to
see how quickly they could get the
Beatles in and out of their concert
venues during the various scrums of
regional Beatlemania.

November 16, 1963

SCENES FROM THE WINTER GARDENS,
BOURNEMOUTH
An otherwise inauspicious venue for an
important moment in the Beatles'
career. This night, no less than three
U.S. networks sent TV crews to cover
the Beatles' concert at the West Country
holiday resort. With word of the group's
remarkable success traveling across the
Atlantic, television was quick to try and
capture it as well as the effect the group
was having on Britain's youth.

November 19, 1963

EMI PRESENTATION
EMI headquarters, Manchester Square,
London. The Beatles attended a special
reception convened by the heads of EMI
to receive a clutch of awards and discs
for their records during 1963. In less than
one year, the Beatles had gone from a
small, provincial dance-hall band to the
top-selling artists in the United Kingdom.

Ringo: "None of us has quite grasped
what it is all about yet. It's washing over
our heads like a huge tidal wave. But
we're young. Youth is on our side. And
it's youth that matters right now."

BEATLES BACKSTAGE AT THE REGAL
CINEMA, CAMBRIDGE
The Beatles spent the night at the
nearby University Arms Hotel after
their show at the Regal Cinema. The
management of the hotel, mindful that
many of their staff might attempt to
secure the Beatles' autographs (or something else), went to great lengths to protect the boys' privacy during their stay.

Memo: The Beatles

As many of you know, the Beatles will be
staying here at the hotel tonight. It will
be appreciated that during their stay they
will not wish to be disturbed. It is strictly
forbidden, therefore, for any member of the
staff to try and obtain their autographs or
invite any friends onto the premises during
the evening or the following morning.
Failure to comply with these instructions
will result in instant dismissal.

November 27, 1963

Performing for Granada TV's *People and Places*. During this particular show, the boys engaged in a hilarious interview with fellow Liverpudlian comedian Ken Dodd. Partway through the broadcast, Dodd comically asked the boys about his own future as a beat artist.

Ken Dodd: "Let's invite suggestions for an earthy name for me, what about one?"

George: "Sod."

KNOWING HIS PLACE
George keeping himself to himself on
the *People and Places* show. On account
of his younger age and still developing
talent, George was by default the "third
Beatle." Not yet confident enough to
fully express himself through his songwriting (George had at this point written only one song that was deemed
good enough to be recorded by the
group), he nonetheless threw himself
into fine-tuning his craft, spending
hours practicing his distinctive sound on
the guitar.

SMILES FROM THE NEW BOY

Ringo caught in a moment of repose during the filming of *People and Places*. Although he had visually assimilated into the group, it took considerable time for Ringo to settle fully into the band, given that the other three had been together as a unit for more than four years prior to his arrival. Nonetheless, as possibly the luckiest man alive, Ringo took it all in stride. Despite his turn in fortunes, Ringo wasn't convinced of the longevity of the group's success, and early on he set some of his earnings aside in the hopes of setting up a small business of his own one day.

Ringo: "I've always fancied having a ladies hairdressing salon. A string of them! Strut around in me stripes and tails, you know: 'Like a cup of tea, Madam?'"

December 2, 1963

THE BEATLES WITH MORECAMBE AND WISE
The Beatles never really seemed at
ease when sparring with variety stars,
although one exception was when they
were with Morecambe and Wise, the
popular British comedy duo. The boys
spent the majority of the day at the
ATV studios in Elstree, Herefordshire,
rehearsing and performing a short
musical set and a humorous skit with
the duo, which included the old music-
hall number "Moonlight Bay."

CHARITY DUTY

After their frantic day recording with Morecambe and Wise, the boys performed a long-standing charity gig at London's prestigious Grosvenor House ballroom in Mayfair. The Beatles were deeply unhappy about honoring this commitment to London's well-heeled society, even if it was for a charitable cause; as a result, they turned in a less than accomplished performance.

John: "If anybody tells us we were good tonight I'll spit in their faces; we were awful!"

December 7, 1963

JUKE BOX JURY

The BBC's output to pop music in 1963 was decidedly minute. As a result, the nation was starved for anything to do with pop, and the audience ratings for *Juke Box Jury* were enormous. This show, a bland attempt to review the week's latest releases in a "hip" format, received a considerable boost when the four Beatles appeared on the judging panel for this week's edition. The recording coincided with a special concert for members of their fan club based north of Birmingham, and so the Liverpool Empire stage was temporarily transformed into a television studio.

David Jacobs (the show's host): "In my time I've introduced people from Sinatra to Crosby, and all I can say is, I am as excited as you are."

THE MORNING AFTER THE NIGHT BEFORE
Meeting the press at Lewisham Odeon,
Southeast London, after the busiest day
of their career to date. A "how long's
it going to last?" mentality dictated
that the group had little time to relax,
lest the bubble burst.

George: "We'll soon be needing pills
to keep going."

December 20, 1963

The Beatles onstage at the Astoria
Cinema, Finsbury Park, in London, for
their first *Christmas Show*. The production, a mixture of skits and music, ran
for 16 nights over December 1963
and January 1964. The host, a young
Australian called Rolf Harris, had the
unenviable task of keeping order as
100,000 possessed Beatlemaniacs passed
through the Astoria's doors during
the run, intent on catching the boys'
attention.

Rolf Harris: "For their spot, the
scream was unbelievable, you couldn't
hear a sound, the Beatles might just as
well been miming out there. All you
could hear was screaming, the whole
audience. It was unbelievable."

REHEARSING AT THE LONDON PALLADIUM
The success of the group's first appearance on television's *Sunday Night at the London Palladium* ensured that impresario Val Parnell was constantly badgering manager Brian Epstein for the Beatles' patronage on his top-rated show. The predictable roar from the fans during the boys' performance led the show's host, Bruce Forsyth, to come up with an idea.

Bruce Forsyth: "We wondered how could we possibly have the Beatles on the *Palladium* show with all this screaming going on because we knew that the fans would get lots of tickets on the night. So I came up with the idea of using boards. So after their second number, Paul ran off and came back with a big board with a little bit of conversation on it: 'It's nice to be on the *Palladium*.' And then John would run off to the other side with another big board saying, 'Yeah, isn't it lovely, Paul?' They loved the idea."

January 12, 1964

ROCKING THE PALLADIUM
Onstage at the London Palladium,
Paul, George, and Ringo rehearse for
their upcoming live appearance on
Sunday Night at the London Palladium.
The group had a strong dislike of mim-
ing, a common practice among many
of their peers at the time, and would
attempt to play live wherever possible.
They played five numbers that evening:
"I Want to Hold Your Hand," "This
Boy," "All My Loving," "Money," and
"Twist and Shout."

January 14, 1964

January 15, 1964

TAKING THE AIR
John and George having a relatively
quiet time on the streets of Paris. The
buildup to their French concerts was
fairly low-key, which afforded the band
some time for meandering around the
French capital prior to their first performance.

Q: "How important is it to succeed
here?"

Paul: "It is important to succeed
everywhere."

Q: "The French have not made up
their minds about the Beatles.
What do you think of them?"

John: "Oh, we like the Beatles.
They're gear."

January 16, 1964

After conquering Britain, the Beatles'
reception in the French capital was a
tad lukewarm. The group was slotted
into a 9-act, 18-day season at the
Olympia Theatre in Paris where the
audience, principally made up of young
men, was considered restrained when
compared with reactions they were
getting in the United Kingdom.

George: "The audiences were a bit
funny, you see. There were more boys
than girls, and we missed the good old
screams. But, you know, there were
quite a lot of shouts."

TOP OF THE CHARTS

Ringo and Paul relax back at the George V Hotel in Paris after their first show at the Olympia. Despite the less than ecstatic response from both crowd and press, they now had greater things on their minds. That night, the news had come through from America that their single "I Want to Hold Your Hand" had reached number one on the Stateside charts. America was in an elevated state of anticipation for the band's arrival, and *Cashbox* magazine was predicting that the Beatles "could change the whole thinking of American companies toward all British records."

Dezo Hoffman (Beatles' photographer): "The news had come through that 'I Want to Hold Your Hand' was number one on the American Top 100. The Beatles couldn't even speak—not even John Lennon. They just sat on the floor like kittens at Brian's feet."

Brian Epstein: "There can be nothing more important than this, can there be?"

January 16, 1964

BRIAN AND HIS BOYS
Away from the madness, Brian and
charges relax back at the George V
Hotel after hearing of their American
success. Brian was never happier
than when he was alone with them,
and was as besotted as any Beatles-
obsessed teenager.

Brian Epstein: "The Beatles have
broken every conceivable entertainment record in England. They are the
most worshipped, the most idolized
boys in the country."

February 5, 1964

BACK FROM PARIS

The boys alight from their BEA plane,
which was hastily inscribed with an
extra "TLES" to garner some cheeky
publicity for the aircraft carriers and
to offset the losses the boys would
incur while in France. Whatever the
merits of their trip to Paris, they now
had America in their sights.

Q: "Looking forward to this American
trip, have you had any reaction over
there? Have you got any fan clubs
going as we speak?"

Ringo: "Well, there's one supposed
to be started and they're getting quite
a good response, you know. Twelve
thousand letters a day."

February 7, 1964

PRIOR TO TAKEOFF

It was becoming something of a tradition for the boys to give a perfunctory press conference before leaving
Heathrow Airport; here, the lads give
a few, slightly nervous words in
between drinks and cigarettes before
boarding their Stateside plane. Despite
the positive signals coming in from the
States, the group was still somewhat
apprehensive about what the reception
would be on their arrival there.

Paul: "Since America has always had
everything, why should we be over
there making money? They've got their
own groups. What are we going to give
them that they don't already have?"

HUSBAND AND WIFE

In a small anteroom at London's Heathrow Airport, John and wife Cynthia face the press for the first time as husband and wife. For months, John's marriage to Cynthia was a carefully guarded secret, Epstein fearing that if the fans got wind of a married Beatle it might precipitate a downturn in the group's popularity. Given the scurrilous nature of a certain section of the British press, the secret was out toward the end of 1963 (with no visible reverse of fortunes). Although Beatle partners were strictly forbidden from attending the group's tour itinerary, Cynthia was allowed to accompany John for their first trip to the States.

Cynthia Lennon: "The day of our departure to America was finally upon us and we were all beside ourselves with the thrill of the whole adventure. I think I must have been the most envied young lady in the British Isles and America that day. I felt like a billion dollars."

February 7, 1964

The Beatles on the steps of the aircraft prior to their departure to America. Although unknown to the boys' touring party, the first of what would be more than five thousand New York Beatles fans were already gathering at JFK Airport in anticipation of their arrival.

Ringo: "There won't be many there. The airport's too far out from the city."

February 7, 1964

MEET THE PRESS
The boys convene a chaotic press conference at JFK Airport. In a room barely able to accommodate one hundred, more than two hundred newsmen and other associated media crammed in to quiz the Beatles.

Q: "What do you think your music does for these people?"

Paul: "We don't know. Really."

John: "If we knew, we'd form another group and be managers."

February 9, 1964

GETTING READY

John rehearsing for the *Ed Sullivan Show*. The anticipation of their appearance was palpable, with the New York theater surrounded by a phalanx of policemen and screaming crowds. There was a minor worry when, during the rehearsals, George developed a sore throat that quickly turned to influenza. With George confined to his bed, the group struggled on as a three-piece with road manager Neil Aspinall standing in for the benefit of the cameras.

Ed Sullivan (inquiring about whether Harrison would turn up for the show): "He'd better be, or I'm putting a wig on myself!"

"NICE TO MEET YOU, MR. SULLIVAN"

Perfect timing was a major factor in the Beatles' success and at no other time was this more the case than in the events leading up to their first engagement on the *Ed Sullivan Show*. By sheer coincidence, the Beatles' arrival at Heathrow, following their riotous tour of Sweden in late 1963, coincided with a visit Ed Sullivan and his wife were making to the United Kingdom. Intrigued by the chaotic scenes at the airport, and after checking out the band live, Sullivan booked the group for two appearances on his show, long before the mighty Capitol Records, EMI's label in the States, launched its massive Beatles publicity campaign on the youth of America. A record 73 million viewers tuned in to see the group's first appearance on Sunday night, February 9. Among them was evangelist Dr. Billy Graham, who even broke his pledge never to watch television on the Sabbath. Interestingly, the crime level in New York City was at an all-time low during the night of the broadcast. The Beatles had enchanted the nation.

Allen Ginsberg: "I started dancing. It seemed that the years of wartime repression were really over, or something was over, and the new era had begun. People were returning back into their bodies unafraid and were celebrating their physical existence—the dance, which is an old human ritual. Everybody was moved to dance."

February 9, 1964

Ed Sullivan: "Yesterday and today, our theater's been jammed with newspapermen and hundreds of photographers from all over the nation. And these veterans agree with me that the city never has witnessed the excitement stirred by these youngsters from Liverpool who call themselves the Beatles. Now, tonight, you're going to be twice entertained by them. Right now, and again in the second half of our show. Ladies and gentlemen, the Beatles!"

February 9, 1964

"THEY'RE HERE!"
The Beatles' onstage set at the Ed
Sullivan Theater. The designers certainly earned their paycheck that day
with a backdrop that imaginatively
exploited this historic moment—the
arrows pointing to the four most
famous men in the Western Hemisphere
perfectly summed up the feeling across
America.

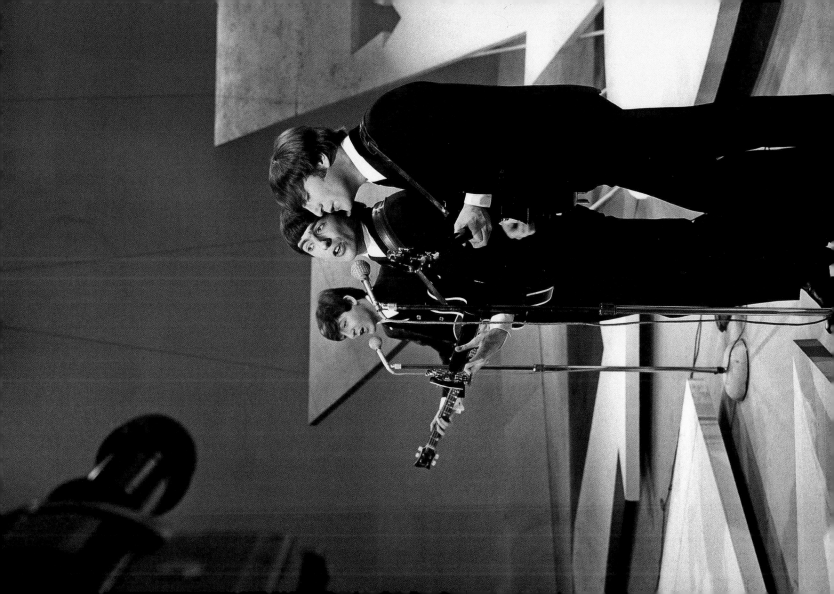

GATHERING AROUND THE MAN
The Beatles' appearance on Ed
Sullivan's show was a milestone in the
history of American broadcasting—
the broadcast garnered the highest
number of viewers of any TV show up
to that time. Prior to their arrival in
the States, the booking that Sullivan
had made was based strictly on the fact
that the group was a U.K. phenomenon; they were considered more a
curiosity than a significant entertainment act. But the events of early 1964
changed everything, and the Beatles
rolled into town as the world's hottest
performers.

February 11, 1964

OUTSIDE THE WASHINGTON COLISEUM
Snow had enveloped the East Coast
for the first few days of the Beatles' stay
in the States, and so the group opted to
take the train to Washington, D.C., for
its first concert on U.S. soil.

Q: "You and the snow came to
Washington at the same time today.
Which do you think will have the
greater impact?"

John: "The snow will probably last
longer."

To give everyone in the 8,000-capacity crowd the best possible view, the Beatles' stage was situated in the center of the arena, necessitating that the group play alternate sides of the stage for several numbers before rotating around to face another side of the arena. Ringo's drum kit, placed on a mechanically revolving dais, actually broke down partway through the show and had to be manually pulled around by the drummer. Ringo wasn't that bothered though, nor was he worried by the hail of Jelly Beans lobbed at the group from adoring fans.

Ringo: "Some of them were throwing Jelly [Beans] in bags and they hurt like hailstones, but they could have ripped me apart and I couldn't have cared less. What an audience! I could have played all night."

February 11, 1964

VIEW FROM THE SIDE

Washington was a tour de force for
both group and audience. Judging
from the surviving film footage—
relayed to thousands via closed-circuit
television—the Beatles gave their all
during the concert; despite the silly
revolving-stage maneuvers, it remains
a highpoint in their performing career.

John: "They are the wildest, you
know? Tonight was marvelous!
Ridiculous! Eight thousand people all
shouting at once. We were trying to
shout louder than them with micro-
phones and we still couldn't beat them.
We thought it would be much quieter.
We thought we'd have to grow on
everybody, but everybody seems to
know us already as if we'd been here
for years. It's great!"

February 12, 1964

One of the conditions attached to the
Beatles' appearance in the loftiest of New
York's concert venues was that no pho-
tography of any kind was allowed inside
the hall. As a result, precious few photographs exist from either of the two
shows; most of the few images that sur-
vive come from the fans' lenses. However,
this shot was taken surreptitiously without lighting, by a professional. To
accommodate the six thousand–odd fans
who'd bought tickets and the scores of
New York's celebrity set intent on attending, a compromise was reached, allowing
a small number of fans to sit at the side
of the stage during the two performances, thereby freeing up some of the
valuable seating.

February 16, 1964

SCENES FROM THE ED SULLIVAN SHOW AT
THE DEAUVILLE HOTEL, MIAMI
Such was the reaction to the Beatles'
first appearance on the *Ed Sullivan
Show*, the highest-rated show in U.S.
television history, that the production
crew traveled to Miami, where the
Beatles were resting for a few days, to
film yet another performance. This
gave them two appearances on Sullivan's
show during their stay in the States.

Ed Sullivan: "These boys are good
musicians. When I finally saw them
play in England, and the reaction, I
said to Mrs. Sullivan, 'These boys have
something.'"

February 16, 1964

PAST THE SUN BEDS . . .
The boys, a Miami police guard, and
road manager Neil Aspinall walk around
the back of the Deauville Hotel in Miami
en route to the hastily improvised TV
set in the ballroom where they were to
film their second appearance on the *Ed
Sullivan Show.* The advertisers, with
the promise of another 70 million–plus
audience in attendance, were squealing
with delight at their fortune.

THESE BOYS

Surrounded by a phalanx of television
cameras, the boys put in a rousing performance of "This Boy" for their
second live Ed Sullivan performance.
Later in the year, Sullivan would follow
the group over to England to record
an interview during the filming of the
Beatles' first movie, *A Hard Day's Night*.
Sullivan's relationship with the Beatles
would endure over the years, the highpoint being his introduction of them at
their historic Shea Stadium concert
(August 15, 1965). The group would
appear live on the *Ed Sullivan Show*
only one more time, but a steady stream
of filmed appearances would continue
to make their way onto his show.

February 17, 1964

THE BEACH BOYS

Initially, the Beatles' first trip to the States was solely a promotional affair, with radio and television exposure the priority. Naturally, given the phenomenal response, other elements were drawn into the Beatles' schedule to satisfy the enormous demand. But the group was adamant that they be allowed a few days' rest and relaxation in Miami to wind down after their endeavors. Epstein, true to his word, allowed the group some quality time in the sun.

Q: "Did you ever have a chance, John, to just get away on your own without anybody recognizing you?"

John: "Yeah. We borrowed a couple of millionaire's houses, you know."

Q: "You could afford to buy a couple of millionaire's houses, couldn't you?"

Paul: "No."

John: "Yeah, we'd sooner borrow them. It's cheaper."

February 17, 1964

IT'S A LONG WAY FROM LIME STREET
John, boots and clothes in hand, makes
a dash from pool to lounge chair during the boys' afternoon photo session in
Miami. The Beatles were still in awe of
the trappings of their success and gleefully lapped up all the attention they
were receiving. Certainly, they'd come
a long way from the days of cadging
bacon sandwiches and cups of coffee in
return for playing in Liverpool's clubs
and bars.

February 17, 1964

TOWELLING OFF

Paul takes a towel to his precious hair.
It was a peaceful few days in Miami
and a welcome respite from the madness they were experiencing everywhere else. Miami offered the group
some much-needed time to reflect on
their amazing success in the States. The
sunny city welcomed the boys to its
warm shores and offered them whatever they needed during their stay.

Paul: "We borrowed these houses,
you see. These people rang up and
said, 'Do you want our house, lad?'
So we said, 'By gum, we do!'"

February 17, 1964

HERE COMES THE SUN
George takes in the Miami air from the Deauville Hotel pool. The group had a long-standing arrangement with *LIFE* magazine for a series of pictures to be taken in Miami, which the group undertook with characteristic glee. These photos have long been regarded as some of the best ever taken of the group during the Beatlemania period.

George: "I think I enjoyed the sun in Miami most of all. You know—healthy."

Q: "You're the healthy one of the four?"

George: "No, but the sun was sort of very healthy."

February 17, 1964

EASY DOES IT

Asleep on a beach chair at the Deauville
Hotel, Ringo keeps the peace as *LIFE*
magazine prepares yet another photo
opportunity. Ringo loved Miami. The
romantic dreams of America he had
harbored long before his initiation into
the Beatles finally came to fruition
with this trip.

Ringo: "Oh, I just loved all of it, you
know. Especially Miami—the sun. I
didn't know what it meant till I went
over there."

Q: "Don't you get it up in Liverpool?"

Ringo: "No, they're finished up there,
you know. They've cut it out."

February 17, 1964

I'LL FOLLOW THE SUN
During these halcyon days of
Beatlemania, the boys languished in
the Miami sun with a close retinue
of friends and colleagues, including
Brian Epstein, Neil Aspinall, and
George Martin.

HEAD BANGERS

During their break in Miami, the boys attended a training session for Cassius Clay, who was preparing for his world-title battle against Sonny Liston. The Beatles were never that keen on sports of any kind, yet it was generally agreed that the photographic opportunity to pitch the world's "most popular" against the self-appointed "greatest" was too good to miss.

Cassius Clay: "Hey, you guys aren't as stupid as you look."

John: "Yeah, but you are."

February 19, 1964

BACK IN THE U.K.

John, with the help of some of London's
finest security personnel, makes his way
to the terminal at London's Heathrow
Airport after returning home from the
States. After an ecstatic reception on
the tarmac, the group would convene
in the pressroom at the airport to be
greeted by the similarly enthused ranks
of U.K. press and television, all eager
to gauge their opinions on their first
visit to America.

February 22, 1964

THEY'RE BACK!
The Beatles attempt to make their way toward Heathrow terminal through what amounted to a scrum of hundreds of journalists and photographers. More than 3,000 fans turned out early in the morning to greet the boys.

George: "It [U.S. tour] was marvelous, you know. Everything. Every bit of it was a knockout."

Q: "What about the taste of the fans over there?"

Paul: "Yeah."

John: "He never bit any."

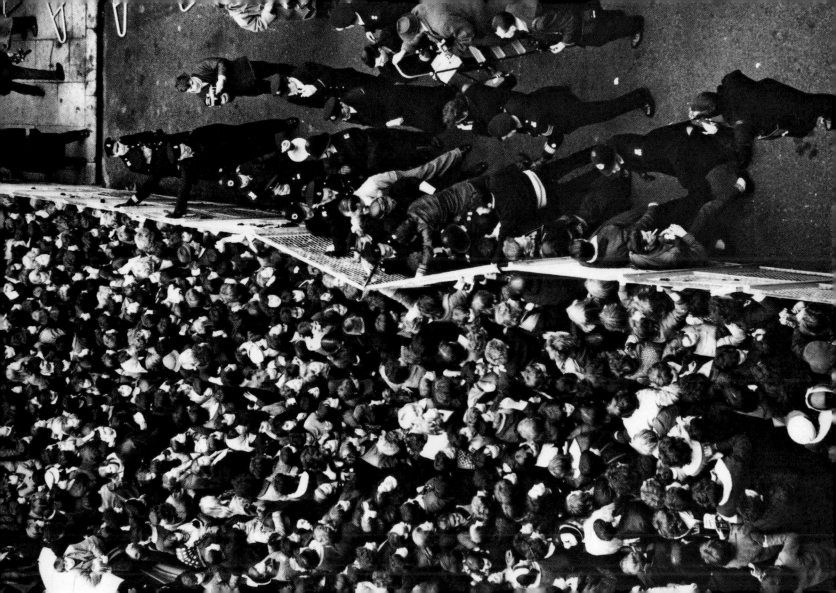

BIG NIGHT OUT

There was to be no letup for the boys after their trip to the States, and just 24 hours following their tumultuous return to Britain, they were back into the hectic round of public appearances and recording. For their appearance on the variety show *Big Night Out*, the boys arrived at London's Teddington studios on a boat and then—equally for the benefit of cameras—climbed into a 1912 Rolls Royce. While en route to the television studio, 16-year-old fan Susan Sims burst through the security cordon with "I Love George" placards pinned all over her jacket and dived into the moving car.

Paul: "I don't think fans are humiliating themselves. I queued up at the Liverpool Empire for 'Wee' Willie Harris's autograph. I wanted to do it. I don't think I was being stupid."

February 23, 1964

The boys take a brief break from
recording *Big Night Out* to greet the
press. As per usual, the group had
to parry the seemingly interminable
questions about the longevity of
their successs.

Q: "Do you think this is a fad?"

John: "Obviously. Anything in this
business is a fad. We don't think we're
going to last forever. We're just going
to have a good time while it lasts."

February 25, 1964

DOOR OF THE KEY

For George's 21st birthday, the
youngest Beatle received 52 sacks
of mail containing more than 1,500
cards and presents from adoring fans,
a sizable portion of which was deliv-
ered to his parents at their Liverpool
home (most were just addressed
"George Harrison, Liverpool").
Among the thousands of letters
adorned with coming-of-age keys,
one thoughtful wag even sent George
a door!

March 1, 1964

With a few moments spare, George arrives outside a London car show-room to pick up his new E-Type Jaguar. Fast cars were one of George's undying passions.

George: "I don't think I've changed. I know we've hit it big, but I don't know if I'll ever be a millionaire. We get two bob from every pound we earn, and that's split four ways—six-pence each. If I miss anything in life now, I don't know what it is, because we haven't got the time, any of us, to think what we are missing."

READY, STEADY, SHOOT!

Interior shooting for *A Hard Day's Night*. Since mid-1963, the Beatles had been pursued to make a motion picture. Making a film was a natural extension of the exploitation package that went into the development of a group's career during the early 1960s. As if the Beatles instinctively knew their longevity was worthy of much better things, they rejected many of the advances from would-be movie moguls until United Artists finally offered them a deal to their liking. On board for the production was director and former *Goons* cohort, Dick Lester, while Liverpudlian scriptwriter, Alan Owen, wrote a story around them as true to their Liverpool sensibilities as was allowable. The Beatles, with no formal training as actors to their name, still managed to adapt to the rigors of filming.

Paul: "It was very hard to just learn a line and say it, because we've never done that sort of thing before. We've always just thought of something and said it, rather than actually read something on a piece of paper. But I think towards the end of making the film, we got the hang of it a little bit more. At first, it was very frightening. It was nerve-racking trying to say these things as though we meant them, because that takes training as an actor. So, you know, we had to try and make it look convincing without having any experience."

March 16, 1964

STEPTOE AND SON

Ringo comes to grips with Paul's mischievous onscreen grandfather, Wilfred Brambell (then better known to TV audiences as the cantankerous Steptoe from the BBC sitcom *Steptoe and Son*), during filming of a key moment in *A Hard Day's Night*. Of all the Beatles, it was Ringo who adapted quickest and easiest to the screen with his natural, sardonic persona winning him considerable plaudits. But, like the other Beatles, he found the interminable waiting on set a strain.

Ringo: "Well, it was a hard two months. It took two months actually to make this film. But, I think I found the biggest drag was when we were just sitting around doing nothing."

March 19, 1964

PURPLE HEARTS
At the Dorchester Hotel for a presentation of the Variety Club Silver
Heart awards for Top Show Business
Personalities of 1963. The boys, on a
morning's leave from shooting *A Hard
Day's Night,* breezed into the dining
room to receive their awards from
Prime Minister (and fellow Scouser)
Harold Wilson, and then wasted no
time leaving. Wilson knew instinctively the value of championing the Beatles
when looking at the mass of first-time
voters reaching the register in time for
the general election later that year.

John: "I get my spasms of being intel-
lectual. I read about politics, but I
don't think I'd vote for anyone. No
messages from any phony politicians
are coming through me."

March 19, 1964

JUST THE TWO OF US
John and Paul enjoying a few seconds
of repose at the Variety Club awards
at the Dorchester Hotel. Their day was
full, even by Beatle standards, with
filming on *A Hard Day's Night* continuing after the presentation, and then
an appearance on *Top of the Pops* to
promote their new single "Can't Buy
Me Love."

March 20, 1964

READY, STEADY, GO

A young Beatles fan puts her head
between the shoulders of policemen
on duty outside Television House,
Kingsway, in London, where the
Beatles were due to perform on the
hugely influential TV pop show *Ready,
Steady, Go!*. The Beatles topped off an
exhausting day with a breezy performance on the show, mixing with the
likes of Alma Cogan, Marvin Gaye,
and Dusty Springfield.

March 23, 1964

MORE AWARDS

More silverware, this time from the Carl-Alan Dance Music Presentation Society. The gongs were presented by Prince Philip and convened at London's Empire Ballroom in Leicester Square. The awards—another two in a seemingly endless recognition of their amazing success—were for Outstanding Group of 1963 and Best Vocal Record for Dancing. Later in the year the prince was famously misquoted as saying that the Beatles were "on the wane." What he actually said was that the Beatles "were away."

Q: "Did you know that the Duke of Edinburgh was recently quoted as saying he thought you were on your way out?"

John: "Good luck, Duke."

George: "No comment. See my manager."

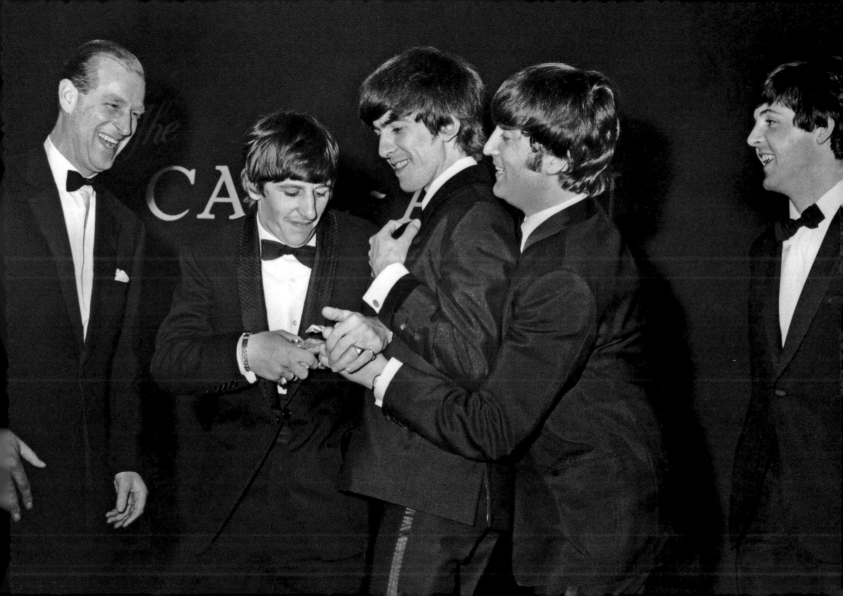

March 26, 1964

(THIS PAGE) ACT NATURAL

A slightly bored-looking Ringo idling a few minutes away before shooting commences at the Scala Theatre in London's West End, where the Beatles were filming concert sequences for *A Hard Day's Night*. Ringo's dry, wry sense of humor was behind his often memorable responses to otherwise inane questions.

Q: "Ringo, why do you wear two rings on each hand?"

Ringo: "Because I can't fit them through my nose."

(OPPOSITE) HAPPY BIRTHDAY!

Costume designer Julie Harris celebrates her birthday with the Beatles and costar Wilfred Brambell on the set of *A Hard Day's Night*. The group had to follow a strict shooting schedule, something they found completely at odds with their nocturnal lifestyle.

George: "You know, we all go out at night. And then suddenly our day was reversed, so that we had to be up at six in the morning, but we still couldn't get the hang of going to bed at night. So we were going out at night and getting up in the morning for the first week or so, and I just couldn't believe it. Six o'clock, somebody dragging me out of bed."

March 31, 1964

A QUIET CHAT

George and John caught having a chat
backstage at the Scala. Although John
and Paul were the principal protago-
nists of the Beatles, their relationship,
while close, had a distinct competitive
edge to it. As a result, John often felt
more comfortable with George than
with his songwriting partner, Paul.

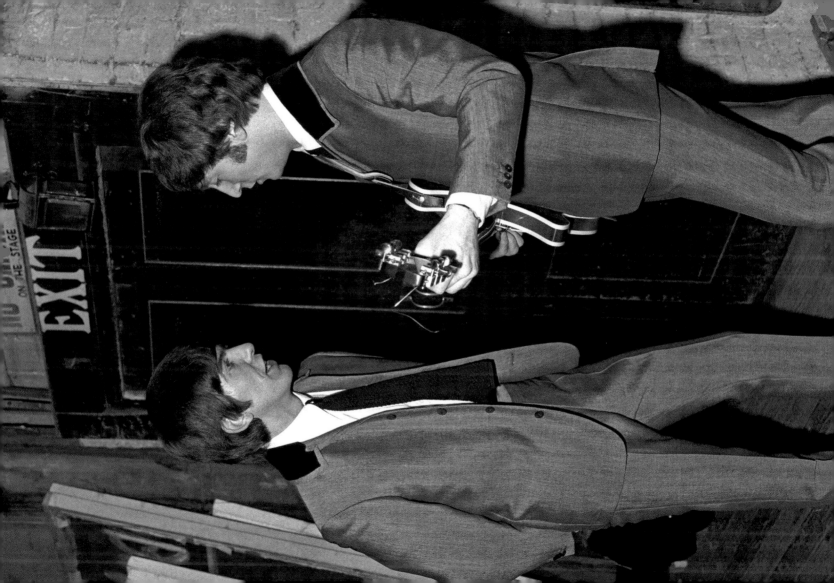

March 31, 1964

PAUL ALONE
Taking a few moments out from the onstage action at the Scala, Paul catches up on the news. At times, Paul displayed a single-minded approach to situations that often resulted in alienating those around him.

Brian Epstein: "Paul can be temperamental and moody and difficult to deal with. He is a great one for not wishing to hear about things and if he doesn't want to know, he switches himself off, settles down in a chair, puts one booted foot across his knee, and pretends to read a newspaper, having made his face an impassive mask."

March 31, 1964

"IT'S ALL GO"

It's all go and the Beatles hit the stage
before a contingent of extras (the
actors' union demanded that the
audience be recompensed for their
"trouble" and so the extras were duly
paid the princely sum of £3.15 [$7.50]
and a packed lunch). One lad cheering
his head off from the stalls of the Scala
was a young Phil Collins, later to make
his own mark on the music world with
Genesis and a successful solo career.

TIME IS TIGHT
Given the hectic shooting schedule for
the Beatles' film, a tailor is brought to
the group's filming location at the
Scala to measure John for a new suit.

Dr. Rennee Fox (writing in
the *New York Times*): "Their fancy
Edwardian clothes suggest a sort of
sophistication that contrasts further
with their homespun style of performance. Much has been made of their
poor, lower-class backgrounds in
northern England. Yet they are accepted by the upper crust, having attracted
the auspicious attention of the Queen
Mother, Princess Margaret, Mrs. Nelson
Rockefeller, and President Johnson."

April 5, 1964

BEARDED AND INCOGNITO
A follicley-enhanced Paul sitting on a
bench at London's Marylebone station
with his onscreen grandfather, Wilfred
Brambell. The Beatles took over the
North London train station for a day's
frenetic shooting on this Sunday in
April 1964. They were filmed running
around the station chased by a mass of
teenage extras and a sizable contingent
of London's bona fide "Beatle People."
Interestingly, the beard-and-mustache
disguise was utilized by Paul on his
occasional outings into the metropolis
during Beatlemania.

YOU'RE NICKED

All four Beatles would have a cameo
written for them for *A Hard Day's
Night*, although none would eclipse
Ringo's moment of glory. Here, the
drummer is seen in a pseudo–police
station at Twickenham studios, trying
to convince the constabulary that he
is the famous Ringo Starr.

Ringo: "I want to see my solicitor."

Policeman: "What's his name?"

Ringo: "Well, if you're going to
get technical."

PATTIE BOYD

The Beatles hugely enjoyed the making of *A Hard Day's Night*, but none more so than George, who, aside from making a very impressive screen debut, met his girlfriend and wife-to-be Pattie Boyd on the set. The pretty model was chosen to play an obsessed teenager trailing the Beatles as they made their way to London onboard a train. George instantly acknowledged her undeniable beauty and immediately made a play for her. Within weeks, they were an item.

Pattie: "I asked them all for their autographs, except for John—I was too scared. When I asked George for his, I asked him to sign it for my two sisters as well, and he signed his name and put two kisses each for them, but under mine he put seven kisses. So I thought, 'He must like me a little.'"

April 9, 1964

A NIGHT OUT

A brief respite from filming *A Hard Day's Night* found George and girl-friend Pattie Boyd having a night out at London's Pickwick Club. The festivities on this night were courtesy of singer Anthony Newley, who was hosting a welcome-home party for him and his then wife's (Joan Collins) return from America.

HONEY, DON'T

Ringo also came along for the Pickwick
bash and spent part of the evening
with the young starlet, Hayley Mills.
During 1964, Paul, George, and Ringo
were the most eligible bachelors on the
planet. It was no surprise then, that the
sight of Hayley Mills talking to Ringo
late at night caused some speculation
from certain quarters of the press as to
the exact nature of their relationship.

Ringo: "I just happened to start talking to her and someone clicked a photo.
Then after that, you know, I'm married off to her, which is silly."

April 15, 1964

A CLEAN OLD MAN

Paul's onscreen grandfather, Wilfred Brambell, hawks his wares outside the Scala Theatre for a key scene in *A Hard Day's Night*. Despite his initial reservation about appearing in a "teen movie," the venerable actor had little difficulty transferring his curmudgeonly persona over to the Beatles' production.

Wilfred Brambell: "They brought me into their generation without me asking. I stepped back and thought, 'No, they're young enough to be my grandsons.' I was cast as Paul's grandfather, and before filming started John said, 'Your part is Paul's grandfather, so stop pretending you're not old enough to be it.'"

April 23, 1964

OUT OF HIS HEAD

After no sleep and a morning's filming,
John arrives at the Dorchester Hotel in
London with wife Cynthia for a Foyle's
literary lunch in honor of his first book
In His Own Write. Brian Epstein was
also present at the event, as was com-
poser Lionel Bart, who was seated next
to John during the luncheon.

RIGHT-HAND WOMAN

A glamorous-looking Cynthia leads
John through the assembled masses of
literary heavyweights to take their
places at the head of the Foyle's table.
It is likely that John would never have
attended if he'd known he was intended
to make a speech; he probably believed
that his presence alone would satisfy
the attendees. After the shock wore
off of being informed that he was to
expand on his literary credentials,
he stood up to make his speech, which
was, in brief: "Thank you very much,
it's been a pleasure."

Cynthia Lennon: "My heart sunk
to my boots. 'John give a speech? Oh
my God, we had no idea.'"

A MIDSUMMER NIGHT'S SCREAM
Rehearsing for the group's TV special, *Around the Beatles*, at Redifussion's Wembley studios. Epstein had wanted the show to be a fast-paced production that would be marketable around the world. For the task, he hired pop-show supremo Jack Good (of *Oh Boy* and *Shindig* fame), and true to his reputation, the American turned in the equivalent of a musical tornado, such was the pace of the production. One of the highlights in the one-hour show was the boys' fairly humorous reading of a tragic/comedic interlude from Shakespeare's *Midsummer Night's Dream*.

Q: "Don't you think you acted strangely on that television program after your return from New York?"

Ringo: "No, not really. We were just having a good laugh, and everyone seemed to enjoy it. So we had a good time, you know. What's the point in being serious all the time?"

The Daily Mirror: "It was noisy and brash. But it was glossy, slick, and professional. It burst out of the screen. None of our pop music shows will be the same after this."

*THISBE: "MY LOVE THOU ART, MY LOVE
I THINK."
PYRAMUS: "THINK WHAT THOU WILT,
I AM THY LOVER'S GRACE."*

Whatever the merits of including a passage from *A Midsummer Night's Dream* in a pop review, the short interlude in *Around the Beatles* did offer some comic relief from the hectic action onstage. With John as a gloriously butch Thisbe and Paul, quite appropriately, cast as Pyramaus, the love-struck male, the Beatles' only venture into classical drama was remarkably proficient, the comedic aspects of the piece allowing them to capitalize on their natural inclination for a bit of fun. (George got the part of Moonshine and Ringo played Lion.)

April 27, 1964

AROUND THE BEATLES
The boys give it their all during
rehearsals for *Around the Beatles*; their
spot at the end of the show was as
frantic and exciting as the rest of the
production. For the first and only time
in their career, the Beatles included a
medley of their hits to date, as well as
a rousing rendition of the Isley
Brothers' hit, "Shout."

April 29, 1964

LARGER THAN LIFE
Prior to shooting off to Scotland for
a couple of gigs in Edinburgh and
Glasgow, the Beatles managed to
squeeze in a few moments at London's
Madame Tussauds to check out their
new wax counterparts. The effigies,
still there at the time of this writing,
were yet another hallmark of the
group's incredible success.

Q: "Don't you feel honored to have
been immortalized in plastic? After all,
there's no such thing as a Frank Sinatra
doll or an Elvis Presley doll."

George: "Who'd want an ugly old
crap doll like that?"

Q: "Would you prefer a George doll,
George?"

George: "No, but I've got a Ringo
doll at home."

April 29, 1964

OCH EYE TH' NOO!
After their whistle-stop visit to gawk
at their wax counterparts at Madame
Tussauds, the Beatles were flown off to
Scotland for a couple of sold-out gigs.
As keen as ever to get the boys engaging in yet another photo opportunity,
the press talked the group into posing
with a few traditional Scottish instruments prior to their first concert
in Edinburgh.

May 26, 1964

BACK FROM HOLIDAY

George and girlfriend Pattie Boyd
arrive back at Heathrow after a
month-long holiday with John and
Cynthia in the South Seas. The press,
eager for any Beatles-related story, had
tailed the party to Tahiti hoping for
any candid moments of the off-duty
Beatles and their partners.

George: "Why can't you just leave
us alone!"

June 5, 1964

JOHN, PAUL, GEORGE, AND . . . ?!
A day before leaving for the Beatles'
European tour, Ringo fell sick at a
photo session and was ordered to rest.
With a series of dates already lined up,
a replacement was quickly lined up
(much to the consternation of George).
Jimmy Nicol, a South London–based
drummer, was drafted to accompany
the group on their tour. Nicol would
continue drumming until Ringo
rejoined them in Australia.

Jimmy Nicol: "Brian had all of the
Beatles, with the exception of Ringo,
who was already in the hospital getting
the swelling down in his throat from
his inflamed tonsils, in an outer office.
In a passing motion, he waved them in
to meet me. I was floored. The Beatles
were actually there to meet me! My
mind was blown. I would have played
for free for as long as they needed me.
I shook all their hands and blurted
out tones of admiration that I think
made them embarrassed. They were
very nice."

June 5, 1964

FILLING THE SHOES
Paul, George, and stand-in drummer
Jimmy Nicol play for Dutch TV at the
Treslong studios in Hillegom, Holland.
Nicol's brief tenure with the band
nonetheless offered him the rare
glimpse of what it was like to be part
of the most famous quartet in the
world. Ten days later he was back on
terra firma, where he quickly fell
into obscurity.

Jimmy Nicol: "I felt like an intruder.
They accepted me, but you can't just
get into a group like that; they have
their own atmosphere, their own sense
of humor. It's a little clique, and out-
siders just can't break in."

June 5, 1964

DUTCH COURAGE

The Beatles' first visit to Holland
included a performance on the top-
rated TV show, *Treslong*. The group,
with Jimmy Nicol standing in, turned
in a great performance, aided by the
close proximity of the audience. They
played six songs—"She Loves You,"
"All My Loving," "Twist and Shout,"
"Roll Over Beethoven," "Long Tall
Sally," and "Can't Buy Me Love"—
before an invasion of the stage by the
ecstatic audience curtailed the show. To
protect the group, road manager Mal
Evans and press officer Derek Taylor
quickly ran to the boys' aid, but the
sheer number of fans made it impossi-
ble to keep them away from the group.
Beatle aide Neil Aspinall briskly inter-
vened and instructed the boys to
hotfoot it off the stage and into the
relative safety of their dressing room.

June 11, 1964

I FEEL FINE
Ringo leaves University College
Hospital in London with Brian Epstein
(at far right, coming through the door)
after being treated for acute tonsillitis.
Epstein had held back from traveling
with the Beatles' touring party so as
to escort Ringo to Australia once he
had recovered.

Q: "Do you think your tonsillitis
might change the group's sound?"

Ringo: "I don't think so, no. Only for
a few days when I can't sing. If you
can call it singing."

June 12, 1964

FELLOW TRAVELER
With actress Vivien Leigh onboard his
Pan American flight, Ringo heads off
to join the group in Australia. Ringo
would have to fly via San Francisco
and Melbourne before finally landing
at Sydney airport to a suitably hysterical welcome.

Q: "You're looking forward to joining
up with them this afternoon?"

Ringo: "It's funny being without
them. Because even when we're not
playing, if we go out, at least two of us
go out together as a rule. So it's a bit
funny being on your own."

June 18, 1964

HAPPY BIRTHDAY!

Paul celebrates his 22nd birthday with
a party following the group's first
Sydney performance. The girls who
attended this somewhat riotous event
were selected from thousands who
entered into a competition setup by a
newspaper to attend the party. Paul's
own brief for the event requested
"champagne and caviar and 15 young
Australian girls chosen for their intelli-
gence and charm."

July 2, 1964

BACK FROM OZ

The boys disembark from a horrendous
23-hour flight to meet the press at
Heathrow following their tour of
Australia. The tour, a critical and
financial success, further cemented the
fact that the group was the show business sensation of the century, with one
country after another falling in love
with them.

July 2, 1964

BACK ON HOME GROUND
Four weary Beatles meet the press at
Heathrow; their spirits were in good
shape despite the long flight.

Q: "What's the rudest question you've
been asked in Australia?"

Ringo: "The rudest was, someone
said to me, 'How are you doing, John?'"

July 2, 1964

HOME SWEET HOME
George greets the press at Heathrow
after the group's tour of Australia.
Although George was the youngest
and most sensitive of the Beatles, this
seemed to matter little, as their friend-
ship was closely bonded irrespective
of age.

George: "It is important to remember that we have been close friends
since school days. A year or two either
way doesn't make the slightest difference in our age group. It would if you
were talking about a George at eight
and a John, age 11, but as a group we've
all had just about the same amount of
experience, and, of course, we've
shared all the same adventures."

July 6, 1964

The Beatles nervously join the lineup for post-movie presentations at the premiere of *A Hard Day's Night* at the London Pavilion Cinema. The special guests that evening were Her Royal Highness Princess Margaret accompanied by her husband, Lord Snowdon. The young, trendy royal couple was rapidly becoming synonymous with celebrity Beatles events; one newspaper even dubbed Margaret the "Beatle Princess."

Cynthia Lennon: "The streets were lined with screaming, cheering fans. London was really lit up with the excitement of the event. When we arrived, I had never seen anything like it before in my life—I had to pinch myself in case I was dreaming."

July 6, 1964

HANDBAGS AND GLAD RAGS
The boys, with their respective parents
and partners, dance the night away at
London's Dorchester Hotel following
the premiere of *A Hard Day's Night.*
The Beatles and their families were on
a high after the star-studded event at
the London Pavilion.

BIRTHDAY "BUMPS"

The Beatles regularly appeared on BBC's weekly chart show *Top of the Pops.* This time it was to preview their new single, "A Hard Day's Night." Normally a one-song-per-performer format was strictly observed, but as always, the Beatles were offered enough time to preview both sides of their latest album. With an extended-play disc also riding high in the charts, the group performed three songs, to the delight of the BBC's management.

Ringo's birthday offered another photo opportunity, and the press happily focused on the Beatles giving their oldest member (now 24) the customary "bumps" (a British birthday tradition). Thousands of gifts were sent by fans, but within the group celebrations were taken very lightly; usually they bought one another gag gifts and weird objects such as pairs of crutches, beef-burgers, and prosthetic limbs.

July 7, 1964

RINGO'S BIRTHDAY

The boys interrupt filming for *Top of the Pops* to give Ringo "the bumps" on his 24th birthday.

Q: "Well, happy birthday, Ringo! Any good presents?"

Ringo: "Quite a few."

Q: "Anything in particular?"

Ringo: "No. The fans sent me a lot of cards and dolls and rings, and that. Oh, I got one funny one from America—a bull ring, off a bull's nose. I don't know if that is an insult or what."

FLYING BEATLES AT THE PALLADIUM

In the space of a year, the Beatles found themselves returning to London's premier variety theater for the third time. On this occasion, they were to perform at a charity event entitled *A Night of a Hundred Stars*. With them during rehearsals was the larger-than-life Zsa Zsa Gabor.

According to press reports, Ms. Gabor was initially going to appear as a magician's assistant, but owing to her fear of enclosed spaces—she was supposed to disappear in a magician's box—she opted for introducing the Beatles onstage instead. The group played a brief musical set and appeared in a short skit, during which they were suspended from the arches of the theater while singing "I'm Flying" from the *Peter Pan* musical.

July 27, 1964

SVENGALI SUPREME

A rare moment of repose for Brian
Epstein as he relaxes in his luxury
Knightsbridge flat before yet another
jaunt abroad with the Beatles (this time
to Sweden). In just two years, Epstein
had elevated himself from provincial
record-shop proprietor to one of the
world's most powerful entertainment
impresarios.

Q: "What's the hardest problem
you encounter trying to manage
the Beatles?"

Brian Epstein: "Well, none really.
But I think traveling around the world
and making arrangements for moving
around is the most difficult thing,
because you don't know what's going
to happen."

August 18, 1964

The Beatles arrived at Los Angeles
airport on the afternoon of August 18,
knowing that for the next three weeks
they would be lucky to find time to
catch their breath. With 32 shows in
24 cities there would be little respite
for the group during this, their most
demanding schedule to date. The
exhausting itinerary took the group,
who by now were beginning to suffer
from chronic Beatlemania, to the edge,
and they vowed never to undertake
such a hectic tour schedule again.

August 18, 1964

PRESS CALL AT THE HILTON
Within hours of their Los Angeles
press conference, the Beatles held
another portal for the media, this time
from the Hilton in San Francisco,
prior to the sell-out concert at the
Cow Palace.

Q: "What do you boys plan to do in
San Francisco other than sleep?"

John: "Sleep."

Ringo: "Just play the Cow Palace,
that's about it."

Q: "You're not going to see the town?"

Ringo: "No, we're not going to see
your beautiful city that we've heard so
much about."

Q: "Why not?"

George: "It'd take too much organization, wouldn't it?"

August 18, 1964

BEATLEMANIA FOR A MONTH

A pensive George ponders the Beatles'
itinerary at the first press conference
of their U.S.A. tour. Out of the four, it
was probably George who was the most
apprehensive about this jaunt. His
own soul-searching was distinctly at
odds with the trappings of stardom,
and given that any time onstage would
be drowned out by overzealous
screaming fans, the month-long tour
was bound to be an ordeal for him.

(THIS PAGE) BY THE REAR ENTRANCE
By now, the Beatles were on to every possible ruse and device employed to gain entrance to their private quarters, so any alternative routes were quickly leapt upon by clever fans. Scenes like this, of intrepid Beatles seekers scaling the rear of the group's Hilton Hotel base in San Francisco, were common in those days.

(OPPOSITE) THE COW PALACE, SAN FRANCISCO
Over 17,000 Beatles fans, beside themselves with ecstasy, kept up a steady cacophony of screams from the moment the group appeared at the Cow Palace, pausing for breath only when the band left the stage some 30 minutes later. Not taking any chances over their beloved auditorium, the authorities erected chicken wire to contain the hordes clustered around the stage. Immediately following the concert, the Beatles boarded a plane bound for Las Vegas and more chaos.

Q: "Why did you start the tour in San Francisco?"

John: "We don't plan the tours. We just say we don't want to go to 'Ba-boo-boo land' and we leave the rest of the world open, and it's all planned for us."

August 19, 1964

ONSTAGE AND IN UNISON
Paul, George, and John give it their all
at San Francisco's Cow Palace. This
U.S. tour had a steep learning curve
for the group and, by extension, the
pop-music industry. Prior to this tour,
the Beatles had been used to playing at
cinemas, clubs, and theaters, usually
with a capacity of no more than 2,000.
Now they were playing to enormous
arenas and stadiums, larger venues
than any act before them had ever
played. Yet, despite the increased frenzy and chaos, the boys would never
outstay their welcome onstage, and
after 12 songs in 30 minutes (25 if they
speeded them up) the band would exit
stage left, usually into some armored or
security vehicle, and escape before the
crowd had time to finish applauding.
Needless to say, the music they made
under these conditions was not showing off their talents to best advantage.

Ringo: "You think, 'What am I
doing?' I'm playing the biggest pile
of shit in the world and people are
standing and cheering, which isn't
good for you."

August 20, 1964

A VIEW OF THE MADNESS

Scenes from the Beatles' stay in Las
Vegas. The Beatles arrived at Las
Vegas' McCarran Airport in the early
hours of August 20, although the time
was hardly a deterrent for the scores of
Beatle fans who had been whipped into
a frenzy by the local DJs in the weeks
prior to the group's arrival. To both
protect and confuse fans, the Beatles'
plane was taxied in without lights,
which was, unfortunately, necessary
to prevent the nightmare scenario of
fans running out onto the runway.

The Beatles' shows at the Convention
Center of the Sahara Hotel were a
complete sell-out, exceeding capacity
(and safety limits) for both performances. The demand for tickets could
have easily ensured a higher return on
the gate, although, mainly due to Brian
Epstein's insistence, the ticket prices
were fixed at a little over four dollars.

August 20, 1964

VIVA LAS VEGAS!
More than 16,000 largely uncontrol-
lable fans saw the Beatles play two
shows in the Convention Center of the
Sahara Hotel in Las Vegas. The Beatles
stayed in their hotel rooms for the
duration of their stay, but the building's management—not wishing to
risk the destruction of their precious
casino by rampant fans—forbade the
group to set foot on the lush red car-
pets. Nonetheless, for publicity purposes,
they did send a couple of slot machines
to the boys' suite so they could be photographed engaging in a spot of
gambling.

August 20, 1964

Thousands of Las Vegas' security
personnel were present for the boys'
performances at the Sahara Hotel.
Judging by this view from the front of
the stage, even the hardiest of Beatle
fans wouldn't have stood a chance
reaching the group. However, later in
the evening, it was reported that two
determined teenage fans would breach
hotel security and wind up underneath
John's bed!

LONG TALL SALLY

Paul launches into his favorite Little
Richard number at the Las Vegas show.
The ballroom had hosted presidential
conventions over the years, but not
even the wildest of political gatherings
could match the excitement of the
Beatles' shows. Such was the demand
for tickets that the management was
forced to set up seating behind the stage.

IF I FELL

John and Paul close in on the microphone during one of the Beatles' more harmonically experimental tracks, "If I Fell." For whatever effort the group put into the song, their performances on this tour were all but drowned out by the pubescent screaming.

Q: "Well, it was said in Las Vegas and in San Francisco that your performance couldn't be heard because of the noise. Now, how do you feel about this? Do you consider it might hurt your future concerts?"

Paul: "It's been going on for a couple of years, you know."

Q: "How many more years do you think it will go on?"

John: "We're not taking bets."

Q: "Have you got any idea? Will it be three? Four? What do you think?"

George: "Till death do us part."

ALL PAUL

Protected by Sin City's finest security, Paul belts it out above the din at the Sahara Hotel. Any fun the group was having up to this point was sorely test-ed when the boys were informed that on certain dates in the Bible Belt region they would be playing to segregated audiences.

Paul: "We don't like it if there's any segregation or anything, because we're not used to it, you know? We've never played to segregated audiences before, and it just seems mad to me. I mean, it may seem right to some people, but to us, it just seems a bit daft."

August 21, 1964

A SNAPSHOT FROM THE EYE OF THE
HURRICANE
Before its show at the 15,000-capacity
Seattle Coliseum, the group relaxed
with friends, fans, and managers in the
confines of its Edgewater Inn Hotel,
situated on the shores of Elliott Bay.
To prevent any invasion of their
beloved hotel, the management had a
cyclone fence installed around the property to keep the fans out. However,
it didn't stop the more adventurous
from swimming over to the hotel and
attempting to climb into the Beatles'
private quarters.

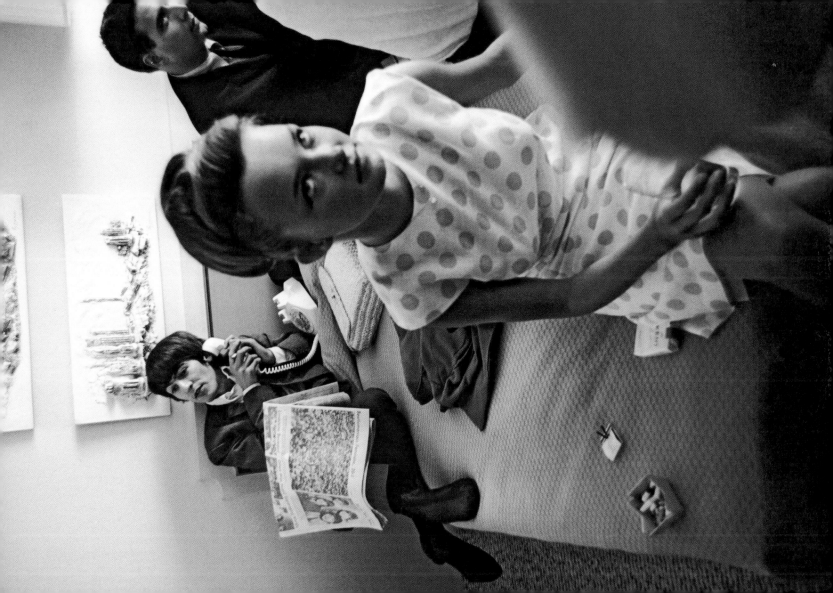

August 21, 1964

SEATTLE CAPTURED

Prior to their storming set at the Seattle Coliseum, the Beatles found a novel way to relax. To help alleviate their boredom, the hotel arranged for fishing rods to be brought to the boys' suite so that they could engage in a spot of fishing from their third-floor window, a pastime that has become a tradition with visiting rock groups ever since.

Q: "Did you get any fishing in today? We heard that you had four fishing poles."

George: "Yeah."

Q: "Did you catch anything?"

George: "No."

Ringo: "Someone on the other side of the lake kept shouting, 'There's no fish in here!' So I sort of got discouraged and pulled my line in."

August 21, 1964

"CAN YOU HEAR US?"
A fan's-eye view from the front of
the stage as police mingled with
Beatlemaniacs during the group's
show at Seattle's Coliseum. The hysterical fans wailed their adoration from
the second the boys hit the stage to
the moment they ran off, where an
armored security van waited to carry
them away.

August 22, 1964

Police struggle to hold back the masses.
Canada had never seen anything like
this—the Beatles' 28-minute performance caused nearly 200 casualties and
scared the wits out of scores of policemen and a few thousand more parents.

Q: "We heard reports that, maybe,
the plane was late and they wouldn't let
you into Canada. Why?"

John: "Because of the hair. You have
to be deloused before you can get in."

August 23, 1964

FOUR ANGELS IN LOS ANGELES
In the City of Angels for the most
prestigious date on the tour's itinerary,
a concert at the Hollywood Bowl.

August 23, 1964

REFLECTION OF THE TIMES

The Beatles played a superb set at the
picturesque Hollywood Bowl. The
venue—with its huge stage fronted by
a giant lake—was renowned for its
acoustics and was therefore deemed a
suitable place to record (for the first
time) the Beatles live. Unfortunately,
the sound from more than 18,000
Beatlemaniacs ensured that the band's
performance would be drowned out
in a torrent of screams. Such was the
disappointment with the recordings
that they would lie untouched in an
archive for more than 13 years until
their eventual release in 1977.

August 23, 1964

Los Angeles had been whipped into a frenzy of Beatlemania by the publicity-savvy media, who tracked the boys' every move before and during their stay in town. The Hollywood Bowl was a rare venue on their tour in that it was used exclusively for musical performances. Its expansive stage and superb acoustics were much to the group's liking.

John: "The Hollywood Bowl, even though it wasn't the largest crowd, seemed so important. It was a big stage, and it was great. We enjoyed that the most."

HOLLYWOOD MEETS THE BOYS
The requests from Hollywood's glit-
terati to meet the Beatles were starting
to overwhelm the group's management. Therefore, it was deemed
appropriate that they accept a request
to attend a garden party held in their
honor by Capitol Records chief Alan
Livingstone. The party, ostensibly a
fundraising exercise for the Hemophilia
Foundation, attracted more than 500
celebrity guests who, after paying
their $25 a ticket, stood patiently on
line to shake the group's hands.

Q: "What about the party yesterday
afternoon that Mr. Livingstone gave?
Was that a highlight for you?"

John: "Well, it was, but it was more
of a job of work, you know. It was
harder than playing. You've just got to
sit on a stool and meet about 300 people of all ages. . . . It is unnatural; it's
natural for us to play and sing. But
it's unnatural to sit on a stool for three
hours and shake hands. But we can do it."

PIE-EYED AND LEGLESS

Delmonico Hotel, New York. After a riotous first night at Forest Hills' tennis stadium, the boys unwind in their Manhattan hotel room. Later that night, Bob Dylan would visit the boys and would introduce them to a substance that would have a profound effect on them for the rest of their careers as Beatles.

Al Aronowitz (journalist): "Each Beatle and Brian [Epstein] had a joint and as we are all puffing, Ringo starts getting high, starts laughing like hell and so we are all looking at him and then we all start laughing at him and then at one another. Brian thought he was floating on the ceiling."

September 3, 1964

ANOTHER DATE, ANOTHER CITY
The Beatles doing the legwork at the
Indianapolis State Fair with two shows
for nearly 30,000 fans. By this point
of the tour, the group was suffering
from the effects of too little sleep and
excessive partying. Any hope that the
group might catch some much-needed
rest after its performances was dashed
as fans repeatedly threw stones at the
boys' hotel bedroom windows. Unable
to sleep, Ringo asked two Indianapolis
State Troopers to drive him to the
famous Indianapolis racing circuit,
where the sleepless Beatle was allowed
to race around the track in the early
hours.

September 17, 1964

A DAY OFF?

Meeting the press prior to the group's
concert in Kansas City. For most of the
tour, Kansas-based promoter Charles
Finley had been pursuing the group to
squeeze in an extra date at Kansas City,
but Epstein and the boys ignored his
advances. In a fit of desperation, and
aware that he'd promised Kansas that
he would deliver, Finley offered the
group $150,000 for a 30-minute show—
an unheard-of fee for a pop concert at
the time. Epstein, aware that history
was in the making, put it to the boys,
who accepted. Finley would be heavily
out of pocket as a result, but he'd kept
his promise to Kansas City. September
17, long pencilled in as a day off from
this, their most hectic schedule to date,
became another concert day.

Charles Finley: "Would you play a
couple of extra songs for Kansas?"

John: "We never do more than 11,
Chuck. You never should have paid all
that money, Chuck." (They would play
one extra song, "Kansas City.")

October 9, 1964

MY GUYS

Mary Wells and the Beatles square up
for a publicity shot for the group's up-
and-coming U.K. tour during a photo
call at Bradford's Gaumont cinema.
Despite the fact that there were seven
other acts on the bill plus a host, Mary
was a coup for the tour, carrying a
considerably high profile after her
enormous worldwide hit, "My Guy."
She was a personal favorite of the
Beatles, so they were bowled over to
have her on the tour.

December 5, 1964

Ringo in his University College Hospital bed in London. Ringo's ongoing tonsillitis caught up with him, and they were finally removed. A special hotline and bulletin board were installed at the hospital to cope with the thousands of calls the staff was receiving from fans inquiring about the drummer's condition. There was even the odd call requesting to collect the infected gland once excised from the stricken Beatle.

Ringo: "The doctors have advised me to take it easy for three or four days. I shall try to sing at rehearsals for our Christmas show. But if I find it hurts, I'll give up."

December 8, 1964

JUST PART OF THE CROWD
Paul and Jane Asher leave London's
Comedy Theatre after seeing Spike
Milligan perform in "Son of Oblomov."
With the 22-year-old Beatle keen to
expand his cultural and artistic knowl-
edge, Paul and Jane were fast becoming
a permanent fixture in London's
celebrity circles.

Paul: "I'm trying to cram everything
in, all the things that I've missed. People
are saying things, painting things, and
composing things that are great, and I
must know what people are doing."

December 10, 1964

Finally released from the hospital,
a relieved Ringo leaves University
College Hospital with Beatles aide
Alistair Taylor to join the rest of the
band in rehearsals for their upcoming
Christmas shows. During the pre-
Christmas dearth of serious news, the
saga of Ringo's tonsils received unprecedented newspaper coverage and had
become something of a national
obsession.

Q: "How did you get on—how did
you get on with the nurses?"

Ringo: "Not so bad, you know! Very
nice nurses in this hospital."

Q: "Were you a model patient?"

Ringo: "You've got to ask the nurses
about that!"

December 21, 1964

BOTH EYES SHUT

George in rehearsals for the Beatles'
1964 Christmas shows. The Beatles
resented having to perform another
long, drawn-out season over Christmas,
especially since they had just played on
a lengthy U.K. tour while attempting
to finish off the recording of their latest album, *Beatles for Sale*—all geared
toward the lucrative Christmas market.
Rehearsals for these shows began on
December 21. Although the Beatles put
in some sturdy performances during
the run, George, more than anyone,
was adamant that these "end of pier"
appearances, which included corny
costume skits, would be their last.

December 22, 1964

THE FIFTH BEATLE

Ringo, Paul, George, John, and Neil
Aspinall backstage at the Hammersmith
Odeon in West London prior to their
second *Christmas Show* season. There
were many contenders to the crown of
"fifth Beatle": George Martin, Brian
Epstein, Pete Best, and Stuart Sutcliffe
were all obvious choices as they all had
played significant roles in the Beatles'
success. But if anyone had had the
most continuous input over the long
term, it was Aspinall, who from the
start shadowed the group's every move
with total commitment, confidentiality,
and unswerving loyalty.

Ringo: "We picked up on Eskimo
gear because Eskimo land seems to
be about the only place we haven't
visited this year."

DOMESTIC BLISS ON THE PISTE
John and wife Cynthia take in the view
from the nursery slopes overlooking St.
Moritz, Switzerland. The couple had
gone to the alpine resort with Beatles
record producer George Martin and
his wife, Judy, for a brief break before
filming started on the Beatles' forth–
coming movie, *Help!* John, aware that
sequences in the picture required skiing
Beatles, may well have been in covert
training.

John: "Both my wife and I did well
because we had a private instructor,
you see, and all the people that sort of
were in big classes were still doing the
same stuff at the end of the two or
three weeks. And we were going down
from the top, so I suppose we were just
above average, because it takes a long
time if you're in a big class of forty,
they can't teach you properly."

EXOTIC HONEYMOON LOCATION?
Ringo finally ties the knot with former Liverpool hairdresser, Maureen Cox. The couple decided against a romantic honeymoon abroad and settled instead for the quaint seaside charms of Hove in Sussex where they announced that they had indeed married the day before. The newlyweds had hoped to spend a week at the house owned by their lawyer, David Jacobs, but word quickly spread; with fans camped outside the house, the couple only stayed for three days before fleeing back to London.

Ringo: "I don't expect anything. I just love being married, and I love my wife. I just want her to be there all the time when I'm there. Now there's no one that can say, 'She can't do this and she can't do that,' you know? If we want to go anywhere or do anything, you know, I'm the boss, we just do it. There's no one to tell us anything else now. It's marvelous."

February 15, 1965

TICKET TO DRIVE

Although the more advanced Beatle in
many departments, John was the last
of the group to pass his driving test.
The press certainly thought it worthy
of news, and John was cajoled into producer George Martin's Triumph while
recording, somewhat appropriately,
"Ticket to Ride" at Abbey Road studios.

February 22, 1965

CHILLY START

The boys brave the early morning chill at Heathrow en route to the Bahamas to shoot exterior sequences for *Help!*, their latest film project. Thousands of Beatles fans were at the airport to give the boys a huge send-off on their first jaunt abroad of the year.

John: "It was very big, because it was a half-day for the school, so there was about eight or ten thousand there. It was like the crowd we got when we got back from America the first time—it was very good."

February 23, 1965

Emerging from the swimming pool at
the elegant Nassau Beach Hotel in the
Bahamas during filming of the Beatles'
second movie, *Help!*

HELP! IN THE BAHAMAS

Whereas *A Hard Day's Night* was pretty much orchestrated by United Artists, by the time their second feature, *Help!*, was conceived, the group was beginning to take much more of an interest in their own affairs. The idea for the film found much favor in the Beatles' camp, and buoyed by the prospect of a James Bond–style romp, the group pitched in its own ideas as to where the film might be shot.

Paul: "I remember one of the first conversations was 'Hey, can't we go somewhere sunny?' It was conceived a bit like that. 'The Bahamas? Sure we could write a scene in where you go to the Bahamas!'"

February 24, 1965

Astride a motorcycle, Paul takes a
break from filming. The budget for
Help! had certainly expanded since the
monochrome expenses for *A Hard
Day's Night.* Director Dick Lester took
full advantage of the myriad of spec-
tacular locations the Bahamian islands
offered, shuttling the group from one
end of the province to the other. Also
taking advantage of the Bahamian sun-
shine was Paul's father, Jim, who came
along for the trip.

Paul: "My dad was here just for two
days after we got in, and he's sunburnt,
and he's having a good time, and he's
swimming again for the first time
in 40 years. And he's gone back to
England now, and he's amidst the snow
of Liverpool. It's snowing like mad in
Liverpool."

February 24, 1965

MORE IMAGES FROM THE BAHAMAS
Although filming in the Bahamas
offered the group a warm start to the
year, the boys were less than pleased
with the way a few crusty colonials
treated them during their tenure there.
As a result, a minor scandal erupted
when, allegedly, the group wasn't
forthcoming in the customary autograph sessions. The Beatles very
diplomatically remained tight-lipped
about their experiences in the Bahamas,
but in later years, John would openly
express his strong opinions about their
stay in the British colony.

John: "The most humiliating experience was sitting with the mayor of
the Bahamas and being insulted by
these fucking jumped-up, middle-class
bitches and bastards who would be
commenting on our work and commenting on our manners."

March 6, 1965

TAKING THE PICCIES
The Beatles clown around at Nassau
International Airport while filming
some scenes for *Help!* The boys poked
some gentle fun at the press and cam-
eramen, who were a constant presence,
stalking the group wherever they went
around the world. Turning the tables,
the Beatles disembarked from their jet
and pointed the camera on themselves.

March 11, 1965

Back from filming, four tanned Beatles
arrive at Heathrow to the early chill
of an English spring. The decision to
shoot first in the Bahamas was ill
conceived as the group returned home
fully bronzed—only then to shoot
sequences in the snow.

March 11, 1965

MY SWEET GEORGE

A healthy-looking George from inside John's chauffeur-driven car as the Beatles' touring party makes a brisk escape from Heathrow. Although George was quite enamored with the Bahamas, he, like the rest of the group, was more than happy to return to Blighty.

George: "I wouldn't mind living in a place like this, with a nice beach, nice sea, and sort of hot climate, but it's so boring after two weeks. But still, I wouldn't mind a place like this for every time you got fed up with the cold in England, you could just fly out here. But I still prefer living in a place like London anytime."

MR. PR

Paul gives his trademark thumbs-up
to waiting crowds at Heathrow. As the
only member of the Beatles predis-
posed toward public relations, Paul
could always be relied upon to smooth
out any situation with the necessary
social graces.

Paul: "To me, that PR thing I just
automatically thought we needed in
the Beatles, to get on and to meet people and the press. So I would do a lot
of that because no one else would. It's
the truth. John would never do it, and
George wasn't into it, and Ringo would
if he liked you, but I'd do it even if I
didn't like you."

March 17, 1965

SKIING BEATLES

Off again to film more scenes for their film, *Help!*, the Beatles find themselves in Obertauern, Austria, a small alpine village outside Salzburg. Here, the boys come to grips with skiing the resort's tricky slopes.

Paul: "We can't act, you know, we're no good."

March 17, 1965

On hand at all times during the filming of these sequences for *Help!* was
director Richard Lester who, aware of
the boys' limited skiing abilities, still
extracted the best from their amateur
attempts at traversing the slopes.

John: "They do so many cuts it looks
as though we're nearly acting, but
we're not."

March 17, 1965

Pattie Boyd (left), Cynthia Lennon
(right), and one of the extras in the film
(center) take the air from the Edelweiss
Hotel in Obertauren. Normally, during
the Beatles' working hours, partners
were strictly forbidden, yet for the filming of *Help!* a rare exception was made.

March 17, 1965

SKI-LIFT OFF

Paul, John, and Ringo take the motorized ski lift to the top of the slope before shooting another take. Although the Beatles appeared in several mountainside sequences, anything other than elementary skiing was left to experienced doubles.

April 6, 1965

April 6, 1965

George takes a few moments out from
filming *Help!* to confer with Beatles
roadie Mal Evans. Unlike *A Hard Day's
Night,* there would be no cameos for
the boys in *Help!,* and although Paul
had a compensatory moment on the
floor with a large boot, the carefully
crafted script made a deliberate
attempt to present them as a unit,
rather than as individuals.

April 11, 1965

For the first time in three months, the Beatles returned to performing live. This concert, at London's cavernous Empire Pool Arena, was honoring the group's recent clutch of awards in the *New Musical Express* Polls for 1964. Handing out the prizes this day was crooner Tony Bennett.

George: "It's a show held by a musical paper. It's something like *Billboard*, it's that sort of thing, only it's called the *New Musical Express*. And they give a concert every year with all the top stars who win awards and just about everybody's on it."

NEW MUSI
POL WIN

April 14, 1965

DOWN YOUR WAY

The word had spread like wildfire among Twickenham's Beatlemaniacs that the group would be filming in the district's Ailsa Avenue for a two-day period, and from early in the morning a sizable contingent of fans had been lying in wait for the Beatles' arrival. When the group did finally appear, it needed all the available assistance from crew and road managers to protect it from the mass of rabid fans.

Q: "Is there anyplace around London that you can get away without crowds, really?"

John: "Yeah, Buckingham Palace. Pretty quiet around there. When she's out it's quite quiet there."

April 14, 1965

DOORSTEPPING

The normally staid Ailsa Avenue in
Twickenham had never seen anything
like it. The district of Twickenham had
no experience dealing with anything
much more than the occasional rugby
scrum and its overexcited supporters
(England's ground was situated nearby), so the Beatles' presence in the area
caused major chaos. As had become de
rigueur for the Beatles, fans were lying
in wait to pounce the moment they
embarked from their chauffeur-driven
limo. Not until the fans were moved
across the street was the group able to
pose trouble free for a few photographs
in front of townhouses 5, 7, 9, and 11.

April 14, 1965

DEAR ELEANOR
Paul chats with fellow *Help!* actor Leo
McKern and leading lady Eleanor
Bron. The actress, who played an
accommodating villain in the boys'
new film, became quite a hit in the
Beatles' circle. She even partly inspired
the title for Paul's lyrical tour de force,
"Eleanor Rigby."

Q: "Eleanor Bron is a pretty good
actress too, isn't she, Ringo?"

Ringo: "Yeah, she's marvelous, you
know. Fantastic."

"BOYS, ARE YOU BUZZING?"
Could be EMI's Abbey Road studios,
but in reality, it's just a clever setup at
Twickenham studios for the benefit of
film cameras. Although it was kept
away from the intrusive noses of the
press, everyone on set was well aware
of what was propelling the Beatles'
jocularity during filming. This scene,
like many others in the picture, was
disrupted by the boys' incessant giggling, courtesy of the "demon weed."

Victor Spinetti (actor in *Help!*):
"They were just laughing and falling
about. . . . I was never involved in
that. I didn't even smoke cigarettes at
that point. I was super cool. I remember John giving me two joints and he
said, 'Smoke these one day when you
grow up.'"

A MOMENT OF TUNING

John takes a brief moment away from filming to check the intonation on his cherished Rickenbacker 330 guitar. *Help!* was altogether a more complex experience than the jollity they'd enjoyed on *A Hard Day's Night*. True, they again had Dick Lester to direct the picture, but the interminable hanging around between shots, coupled with the implausible script, wreaked havoc on their short attention spans. Visually, the film itself had its moments; many years later, John credited the picture as an early precursor to cinematic pop art.

John: "Well, it was 1965. The movie was out of our control. With *A Hard Day's Night* we pretty much had a lot of input, and it was semirealistic. But with *Help!*, Dick [Lester] didn't tell us what it was about . . . though I realize, looking back, how advanced it was. It was a precursor for the *Batman* 'POW! WOW!' on TV, that kind of stuff."

April 30, 1965

YOU'RE GOING TO LOSE THAT GIRL
Ringo casts a beady eye from his drum
stool during another break in filming
Help! This sequence would require a
drumming Ringo to disappear through
a hole in the studio floor, as a band of
religious fanatics desperately tries to
acquire one of his trademark rings.

May 7, 1965

"I KNOW YOU LIKE A SMOKE PAUL, BUT ..."
Interior shooting had all but finished,
but some shots required Paul, seen here
among larger-than-life everyday
objects, to battle his way around the
floor of the Beatles' flat. Incidentally,
the boot seen here dwarfing Paul was
transferred to John's house in Weybridge,
Surrey, soon after filming, where it
stayed until his departure in 1968.

May 11, 1965

Filming at Cliveden House in
Berkshire. The group took over the
sumptuous manor to shoot the final
scenes in *Help!,* with the famous house
doubling as Buckingham Palace. This
two-day shoot provided a couple of
days of tranquillity for the boys, and
even allowed them a spot of relay
racing against the film crew between
takes. During their stay at Cliveden,
their as-yet-unnamed film finally
received its title from director Dick
Lester.

George: "Well, Dick sort of slowly
went up to us, one at a time, punching
us, saying, 'It's going to be called *Help!*'
And we said, 'Yeah, that's a great idea,
Dick, sir, sir. We'll call it that.' And
that's how it all came about."

May 24, 1965

FESTIVAL HOLIDAY

With the shooting of *Help!* finally
completed, John and Cynthia escaped
to the south of France to attend
the annual Cannes Film Festival.
Accompanying them on the trip were
director Dick Lester and producer
Walter Shenson.

June 3, 1965

GET THE KNACK

John, Ringo, and George, with their
respective partners, and manager
Brian Epstein, attended the premiere
of Dick Lester's latest film, *The Knack*,
at the London Pavilion Cinema (Paul
was away on vacation). Since his work
with the Beatles, Lester had proved to
be one of the hottest film directors in
the world.

"MEMBERS OF THE BRITISH EMPIRE"
John and George relax in front of
John's palatial home at St. George's Hill
in Weybridge, Surrey. Earlier in the
day it was announced that the Beatles
had been awarded the MBE, a lowly
award given for "services to the country." In the Beatles case, this meant the
extraordinary amount of cash their
fame was generating for the country.
But its bestowal in 1965 upon something as ephemeral as a pop group was
unprecedented. Although the band had
known for some weeks that it was in
line for the honor, elsewhere it was a
closely guarded secret and all information had been embargoed until the
morning of June 12, at which point the
world's press converged on the group
for its reaction. John's evident embar-
rassment on receiving such an honor
was typified by his initial absence at
a press conference at Twickenham studios, resulting in a frantic Brian Epstein
personally retrieving the errant Beatle
from his home.

Q: "What does it mean to you?"

John: "I don't know till I get it. I'll
read about it and see what it is, really,
'cause I'm not sure what it is. I only
know what I read in the papers."

George: "I didn't believe it at first.
But then when they sent me all bits of
paper saying that, and you lot wrote
it in the papers, well, you had to
believe it."

July 4, 1965

IF THE CAP FITS . . .

Returning from a European tour that
had taken the band to France, Italy, and
Spain, the Beatles arrive to a typically
hysterical reception at Heathrow.
During the stint in Spain, John was
especially taken with the vast array of
hats presented to the group, enough
to wear a few onstage during their
shows there.

July 13, 1965

The usually well-oiled Epstein office had made a bit of a blunder regarding an important ceremony that John and Paul were due to attend. On the morning of July 13, it was noticed that neither Beatle had been told that they were expected to appear at London's Savoy Hotel to pick up a clutch of prestigious Ivor Novello awards. As a result, several frantic calls had to be made. John—mornings not his forte—didn't bother to pick up the phone, while Beatles aide Alistair Taylor had to badger Jane Asher's mother to wake Paul up from his slumber (Paul was then residing at his girlfriend's London house). Paul did eventually appear at the gathering some 45 minutes late and took his place next to famed talk-show host, David Frost. Despite the late arrival, he had a priceless quip regarding the stream of medals being handed back after the group's MBE investiture. (Many recipients, among them war heroes, felt that the MBE presentation to the Beatles "devalued" their honor.)

Paul (on receiving the award): "Thank you. I hope nobody sends theirs back now."

July 29, 1965

HELP! IS AT HAND
Beatlemania takes over Piccadilly
Circus. Thousands of fans crammed
the streets surrounding the London
Pavilion Cinema to get a glimpse of
the Beatles arriving for the opening
night of *Help!*

BEATLES PRINCESS

The protocol for the *Help!* premiere was pretty much a carbon copy of opening night for *A Hard Day's Night*, with (yet again) Princess Margaret and Lord Snowdon undertaking the royal duties for the evening.

John: "You don't get bored, because so many different things happen, like MBEs or premieres, and they're all different, you know, so soon as you start getting bored with something like a tour, the tour's over, and something else starts. So you don't get a chance to get bored."

July 29, 1965

THE BEATLES

HELP

also starring

LEO McKERN

ELEANOR BRON VICTOR SPINETTI ROY KINNEAR

produced by WALTER SHENSON   screenplay by MARC BEHM & CHARLES WOOD   story by MARC BEHM   directed by RICHARD

A WALTER SHENSON SUBAFILMS Production

EASTMAN COLOUR

UNITED ARTISTS

ROYAL WORLD PREMIERE

in the gracious presence of
HER ROYAL HIGHNESS THE PRINCESS MARGARET, COUNTESS OF SNOWDON
and THE EARL OF SNOWDON

Sponsored by The Variety Club of Great Britain
to aid THE DOCKLAND SETTLEMENTS and THE VARIETY CLUB HEART FUND
on

THURSDAY 29th JULY 1965

at the

LONDON PAVILION

Printed by
L. Delow & Co. Ltd.,
1, Southwark Bridge,
London, S.E.1

August 13, 1965

BOUND FOR THE STATES

The Beatles' touring party wanders onto the tarmac at Heathrow for the start of their third U.S. tour. There was a premium attached to this series of dates; it was reported that each Beatle had been insured for £2 million for the duration of the tour. Although they were performing half as many dates as on their previous jaunt around the States, they would in fact play to more fans due to Epstein's desire for the group to play enormous stadiums and arenas to cram in as many fans as possible.

Ringo: "We like our fans, we love what they do. The thing is, all these people who say they shout and scream and 'sbad, but it's not. We like them shouting and screaming, as long as they're having a good time."

August 13, 1965

BEATLES U.S.A.

Airline companies were literally falling over themselves to have the Fab Four fly on their planes during the height of Beatlemania. Following the lead from Pan Am and British European Airways, Transworld Airlines laid on a presentation of specially designed in-flight bags, combining the company's logo and the Beatles' name, for the group's third trip to the States. Seen here leaving the terminal in London, the group collects its travel bags from the daughter of a TWA executive. In the touring party are road manager Neil Aspinall and *Melody Maker* journalist Ray Coleman.

August 14, 1965

John pictured in rehearsals for the *Ed Sullivan Show*. The Beatles spent their first full day in New York rehearsing for an evening performance on the show. John had taken to wearing a pair of mirrored sunglasses he'd picked up in Cannes, France, during his visit to the annual film festival a few months earlier. The shades had the added benefit of keeping any prying eyes from spotting his occasionally bleary orbs.

John: "They're just sort of ordinary sunglasses, only they've got a mirror on one side, so nobody can see in."

CHICAGO, CHICAGO!
The Beatles arrive in Chicago for two shows at the White Sox ballpark, Comiskey Park. Although the Beatles had the privilege of a specially chartered plane, traveling to and from shows was mentally and physically draining for them.

Ringo: "The traveling knocks you out in the end. You sort of get fed up with sitting on planes and in cars, and you want to just sit down for a year."

August 20, 1965

A swift "meet and greet" for the press at Chicago's Comiskey Park. Press conferences had become something of a free show for anyone who could talk their way into the gatherings, and as a result, the questions started spiraling into the realms of stupidity.

Q: "Last summer . . . a doctor said that the Beatles were instruments of the Communists' propaganda [and] that you were softening up and corrupting America's youth."

John: "Yeah."

Q: "What did you say to that?"

Ringo: "Watch out next year."

August 20, 1965

The Beatles emerge from the players'
enclosure to an overwhelming roar, a
cacophonous sound that would last
until the group left the stage. The
Beatles' 1965 tour included quite a few
arenas on its itinerary and would gross
a record one million dollars. Not that
the Beatles were in the slightest bit
interested in being solely an eight-
legged cash machine. Even in 1965,
Ringo had his eyes set way beyond the
confines of a performing Beatle.

Ringo: "I don't think I'll want to be
going onstage when I'm about 30 or
something, playing. I hope that eventually we all move into films."

STANDING IN THE STANDS

Although it may look as though the group is playing to an empty stadium, the setup at Comiskey Park required the band to play at the rear of the field amongst the empty seats. Despite the remote setting, more than 25,000 fans packed into the arena to watch the Beatles' afternoon set, while another 37,000 attended the evening session. The Beatles' paycheck for around an hour's work? $155,000.

August 20, 1965

Playing his cherished Rickenbacker
guitar, John belts it out onstage at
Chicago's Comiskey Park. Since *A
Hard Day's Night* John had enjoyed
wearing a series of caps. Originally
designed as a female accoutrement (his
first was given to him by fashion doyen
Mary Quant), it was instantly copied
by fans across the globe and became
known as the "John Lennon Cap."

August 20, 1965

PERFECT MATCH
Paul and George close in for a harmony
during their performance in Chicago.
Paul's left-handed bass playing allowed
George and him to straddle the micro-
phone while supporting John's singing.

August 20, 1965

ROCKER

Paul moves in to the microphone for a
solo moment at Chicago. Paul was
always the keenest and most energetic
stage performer of the group. Typically,
the Beatles would end their set with a
song from Paul, usually pulled from his
vast repertoire of vintage rock 'n' roll
numbers. During their 1965 tour, Paul
decided to close the sets with a new
composition he had written in homage
to the genre, "I'm Down."

August 20, 1965

The boys leave the stage after their
riotous matinee performance at
Comiskey Park. Surrounding them is
the usual bevy of local radio DJs who
stirred the crowd into a frenzy prior
to the group's arrival onstage.

September 2, 1965

WELCOME BACK

Despite the amazing reception the Beatles received in the States, the boys were still overwhelmed by the turnout upon their arrival in the early hours back at Heathrow. "They deserve the MBE more than us," quipped Paul as they made their way to a chauffeur-driven limousine. Although performing in England would come to a stop within eight months, the group was upbeat about another tour in the States the following year.

George: "It's almost definite that we'll be back around the same time next year. And so if you didn't see us this time, maybe you'll see us next time if you want to, and I hope you do, and all those who don't want to see us . . . never mind."

September 13, 1965

IT'S A BOY!

Ringo celebrates the birth of his first
child, Zak, outside Queen Charlotte's
Maternity Hospital in London. The
second of the Beatle children (Julian
Lennon being the first), Zak certainly
inherited his father's drumming prowess,
which showed up in later years, despite
his father's initial discouragement of the
idea of his becoming a drummer.

Ringo: "Oh, I don't mind him joining
a group, just don't play drums. You
know, all that carrying them around
and everything before you make it, it's
a drag."

September 22, 1965

STARR CHILD
A week after the birth of Zak, Ringo
and Maureen (barely visible behind
Ringo) leave the hospital to go home as
a family. The birth of Zak was a little
problematic, as he was one month
premature, and so Maureen and child
were required to spend a little more
time in the hospital than originally
planned.

Q: "Has he made any musical noises
yet?"

Ringo: "He's shouted out a bit . . .
'Get them press men out of here!'
and all that."

October 26, 1965

George and Paul flash a smile to
the press as they make their way to
Buckingham Palace to collect the
Beatles' MBEs. Although it appeared
(given the column space) as though
the ceremony was exclusively for the
Beatles, it was not, as some 178 other
recipients were also present to collect
their awards from the queen.

Paul: "Some fella was just saying you
have to have top hats. I hope you don't
have to have top hats."

Q: "Will you all wear top hats?"

Paul: "Well, we can carry them . . .
have white rabbits coming out of
them."

Q: "And what about the hair?"

Paul: "What about it?"

Ringo: "We'll put that in the top
hat as well."

October 26, 1965

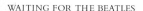
WAITING FOR THE BEATLES

Since the early hours of the morning,
more than 4,000 Beatles fans had
congregated outside the gates of
Buckingham Palace for a glimpse of
their idols. Despite having experienced
numerous royal weddings and corona-
tions, the authorities hadn't seen
anything quite like this. Extra police
were put on duty to protect the royal
quarters from the most zealous of
Beatlemaniacs breaching the palace's
defences.

October 26, 1965

MBEatles

After a slightly nerve-wracking audience with the queen, all four Beatles
make their way from the throne room
to the courtyard for a quick breather
and a cigarette. Behind them to the left
are Beatles manager Brian Epstein and
Evening Standard reporter Maureen
Cleave.

COURTYARD QUIPS

The Beatles show off their MBE awards in the courtyard of Buckingham Palace. The press was keen to find out what had transpired between Britain's trendiest and cheekiest foursome and the monarch.

Paul: "The man shouted out, 'George Harrison, John Lennon, Paul McCartney, and Ringo Starr.' And 'Starr' was the cue for us to walk forward, left foot first—it was just like a show!"

Ringo: "Then we bowed and then we walked to the queen, then we walked back and bowed and then walked away."

John: "Left foot forward."

October 26, 1965

FIRST REACTIONS

The Beatles parade their new official
decoration to the world's press from
the foyer of the Saville Theatre on
London's Shaftesbury Avenue. Lennon
was uncharacteristically buoyant about
the award that day, although he would
vent his true feelings in later years.

John: "You know, before you get an
MBE, the palace writes to you to ask if
you're going to accept it, because you're
not supposed to reject it publicly so
they sound you out first. I chucked the
letter in with all the other fan mail until
Brian asked me if I had it. He and a few
other people persuaded me that it was
in our interests to take it."

VAGUE AND OBTUSE

The Beatles with new MBEs meet the
press reception at Saville Theatre (the
lease of which was recently purchased
by Brian Epstein). Some years later,
John would cheekily undermine the
occasion when he remarked that the
group had smuggled a marijuana
reefer into the palace for a smoke before
the investiture ceremony. Although this
claim was denied by the other Beatles
in later years, John certainly seemed
otherwise "occupied" when talking
to the press immediately after their
presentation.

John: "She [the queen] said to me,
'Have you been working hard lately?'
And I couldn't think what we had been
doing, so I said, 'No, we've been having
a holiday.' But we'd been recording,
but I couldn't remember that."

November 23, 1965

DAY TRIPPERS

John and Paul take a breather between takes for a promotional film insert. Internally the group had (for this period, at least) a rare conflict of interest over the Beatles' next single release. Two numbers, "We Can Work It Out" and "Day Tripper," had been recorded as the respective A- and B-sides of their next record release. Initially, "We Can Work It Out" made the cut, but John vociferously argued the case for "Day Tripper." A compromise was reached, and the first record was released as a "double A-side"—a highly innovative step for the time. The buying public certainly had no arguments with the concept, and the song shot straight to the number-one position across the hit parades of the world.

George Martin: "After we gave both titles to EMI, the boys decided they preferred 'Day Tripper,' but both sides are extremely good and worth a lot of plays."

November 23, 1965

STICKS AND STONED

A wry image of Ringo from the filming of the promotional video to accompany the Beatles' new single release, "Day Tripper." The set designers had their work cut out (literally) that day, as Ringo started out drumming against the image of an old World War I airplane, only then to exchange his sticks for a saw and proceed to cut the backdrop to pieces!

November 23, 1965

The boys take a brief moment to relax
during their busy day of filming. This
particular shot comes from a video
shoot for "Help!," John's first song to
deal with experiences outside of the
boy-meets-girl theme, and a reflection
of the inner turmoil he was going
through at the time.

John: "When 'Help!' came out in
1965, I was actually crying out for
help. Most people think it's just a fast
rock 'n' roll song. I didn't realize it at
the time; I just wrote the song because
I was commissioned to write it for the
movie. But later, I knew I really was
crying out for help. It was my fat Elvis
period. You see the movie: He, I, is
very fat, very insecure, and he's completely lost himself. And I am singing
about when I was so much younger
and all the rest, looking back at how
easy it was."

December 1, 1965

KEEPING AN EYE

Paul and John cast a beady gaze over a
reel-to-reel tape recorder. The setup
was part of a TV special dedicated to
their amazing songwriting talents.
The show, *The Music of Lennon and
McCartney* (also featuring appearances
by Billy J. Kramer, Henry Mancini, and
Marianne Faithful) was shot over two
days at Granada studios in Manchester.
The show's producer, Johnny Hamp,
had devised the concept. Hamp played
a small but important role in the
success of the Beatles, being the first
director to capture the Beatles on film
back in 1962.

December 1, 1965

COMPETING BUDDIES
John and Paul share a quick smoke
during a break from filming their
television special. The program was an
enormous accolade for John and Paul,
then just ages 23 and 25, respectively.
The competitive struggle that existed
between them, while friendly, also
inspired their finest moments.

Paul: "There was amazing competition between us, and we thrived on it.
Those early years, the competition was
great. It was a great way for us to keep
each other on our toes."

December 1, 1965

"IT'S FOR YOU"
Paul and John share a brief moment
with Mersey buddy Cilla Black at
Granada studios during the recording
of *The Music of Lennon and McCartney*.

Paul: "The thing is that if they do our
songs, and do them differently, then,
I think it's better. . . . If they do the
same arrangement, it's their fault, you
know? They shouldn't really do the
same arrangement."

John: "It doesn't matter if they do
them, because it never harms us. . . .
It doesn't seem to harm our sales
too much."

December 1, 1965

UNDER THE SCAFFOLD
John and Paul caught checking out the
art on offer during the filming of their
television special. In addition to the
musical heavyweights paying homage
to the remarkable writing skills of John
and Paul, the Beatles also performed,
choosing to play both sides of their
new single. It's interesting to note that
for the sequence dedicated to the track,
"We Can Work It Out," it was discovered that no keyboard, an integral part
of the song, was available. So, in desperation, a harmonium was filched
from the TV set of the popular U.K.
soap drama, *Coronation Street*, and
absorbed into the group's setup. (*Coronation Street* was being filmed in the same
studios.)

December 1, 1965

SOME HELP FROM OUR FRIENDS

Despite the fact that John and Paul's
TV show was exclusively designed to
extol their phenomenal song-writing
talents, for their own slot in the finale
of the star-studded bill, they needed a
little help from their friends. So for
"Day Tripper" and "We Can Work It
Out," George and Ringo took their
respective places on guitar and drums
with their remarkable partners. Only
in later years would George (and to a
lesser extent Ringo) eventually discover
their not inconsiderable talents as major
composers in their own right.

Q: "Are you more confident about
songwriting these days?"

George: "You get more confident as
you progress. John and Paul's standard
of writing has bettered over the years,
so it's very hard for me to come
straight to the top on par with them."

December 1965

Some of London's finest art designers put this set together. This photo session, which was intended ostensibly to illustrate the program for the boys' next American tour, provided some fine examples of the group's startling uniformity—a paradox considering their strong individual personalities, but not lost on some of the commentators of the time.

Dr. Jonathan Miller: "There is something magical and sinister about repetitive siblings. Mythology is very strong on them. The Beatles inspire terror, awe, and reverence. I had no idea they looked so similar—just marginal differentiations on an identical theme. And with that hair they remind me of [John Wyndham's] Midwich Cuckoos."

December 1965

ANARCHY IN HAMPSTEAD
At the end of a photo session—during
which the Beatles played with various
Eastern instruments, posed with an
Afghan hound, and held up copies of
their LPs—the group smashed the
polystyrene set to pieces in a primitive
display of auto-destructive art, all, no
doubt, egged on by the photographer
Robert Whitaker.

December 10, 1965

HAMMERSMITH ODEON

Ringo taking a few moments out to rehearse for the group's last tour of the U.K. Despite the drummer boy's miserable-looking expression in this photo, he was never happier than behind the drums, and although he had tried out a few other instruments, it was "the skins" that finally won him over.

Ringo: "It was in my soul. I just wanted to be a drummer. I didn't want to be a guitarist. I didn't want to play bass. I wanted to be a drummer, and that's how it is. My grandparents played mandolin and guitar and gave me their instruments, and I just broke them. I had a harmonica; I dumped it. We had a piano; I walked on it. I was just not into any other instrument."

December 10, 1965

Although it was never publicized at
the time, the Beatles U.K. tour in
December 1965 turned out to be the
last trek around their native country.
This night, the group was back at the
Hammersmith Odeon in London for a
solitary evening's performance. The
Beatles' shows in the capital (they
played another date at the Astoria in
Finsbury Park) were a riotous success
and dispelled any notion that
Beatlemania had evaporated.

The Carnival of Light, 1966–1967

"We've all come together along the same path. We've been together a long time. We learned right from the beginning that we're going to be together. We haven't really started yet. We've only just discovered what we can do as musicians, and what thresholds we can cross. The future stretches out beyond our imagination."

—George Harrison

"Young people get inspired by people who talk honestly to them. I think if they believe us on some things, it's because we can say it like they would think it . . . because we're exactly the same and we don't pretend to be anything better than we are."

—Paul McCartney

"I often think that it's all a big conspiracy, that the winners are the government and people like us who've got the money. That joke about keeping the workers ignorant is still true."

—John Lennon

"We can't do a tour like we've been doing all these years, because our music's progressed and we've used more instruments. It'd be soft us going onstage, the four of us, trying to do the records we've made with orchestras and, you know, bands and things."

—Ringo Starr

January 21, 1966

THREE DOWN . . .

They were all smiles as George finally married his girlfriend, Pattie Boyd, after a two-year courtship. The ceremony itself was a modest and brief (seven-minute) affair, taking place in the morning at Epsom Registry Office, Surrey. George had two best men that day: Brian Epstein and the sole Beatle bachelor, Paul. Pattie's proud mum sits at the front of the wedding party with George's parents to the rear.

George had met the pretty model on the set of *A Hard Day's Night* in which she played the role of an obsessed teenager. She initially felt it was John who paid her the most attention, but it was George who ultimately fell for her good looks and sweet charms. However, her initial response to his advances was somewhat out of step with most teenagers around the world.

George: "I asked Pattie out when we were making the film, and she said, 'No!' which [was] very embarrassing at the time, but it all worked out right in the end."

January 22, 1966 (this page)   *Early February 1966 (opposite)*

(THIS PAGE) KISSES AND CUDDLES

The happy couple met the press the day after their wedding. A fairly chaotic press conference ensued with the cheeky newsmen requiring plenty of postmarital kisses for their lenses.

Q: "Well, how do you feel about all this public kissing that you've been subjected to here today at the requests of all these newsmen? Does it embarrass you?"

Pattie Boyd: "Not really, this is my husband now, so it doesn't matter."

(OPPOSITE) IF I NEEDED SOMEONE

George and Pattie spent some quality time in the Bahamas for their honeymoon. With three Beatles now locked in matrimony, there was some spirited speculation about whether the appeal of the group would be diminished.

George: "I don't really think it'll affect it all that much because—well, we proved it, really, when Ringo got married. You're bound to lose a certain amount of fans, but I think the majority of fans realize by now that we've got our lives to lead, and I think they're just as equally interested in the music as they are in us."

LOVING FLAME

Honeymooning together in the Bahamas, George and Pattie put on a display of their love. The couple was the epitome of 1966's swinging London scene—trendy, young, wealthy, and supremely talented in their respective vocations. Pattie had had her own successful career as a model prior to meeting George, and although she cut back her schedule to make time to be with her husband, she still continued to do a few choice jobs as they arose. One thing she hadn't bargained for was the continuing interest in George from overzealous fans.

Pattie Boyd: "I can't get over the fans always hanging round the house, even now. . . . They got into our bed-room the other day and stole a pair of my trousers and George's pyjamas."

Early February 1966

TOGETHERNESS
George and Pattie on their honeymoon. As a Beatle partner, Pattie was
forced to face the wrath of the world's
females.

Pattie Boyd: "They were doing their
Christmas show at Hammersmith. . . .
I scraped my hair back so that I would
look completely different and no one
would recognize me. I don't know how
anyone did, but a few did and started
punching me."

February 17, 1966

BUFFET SUPPER

The Beatles were frequent visitors to London's Saville Theatre where manager Brian Epstein was the leaseholder. On this particular night, John, Ringo, and their respective partners had attended the premiere of Epstein's first (and only) directorial effort: a reading of *A Smashing Day* by Alan Plater at the nearby New Arts Theatre. They convened back at the Saville for a celebration of their manager's newly found direction.

March 25, 1966

GAZING AT THE SHUTTER

A rare moment of repose for John during a photo session in Chelsea, West
London. Now that the content of the
Beatles' lyrics was mining deeper and
more profound topics, commentators
were looking for explanations as to the
significance of the boys' current
spoken-word oeuvre. John, who could
be relied upon to be outspoken, gave a
series of highly personal interviews
during 1966, which fell out of the
frame of previous conversations and
were at times brutally honest.

John: "I want the money just to be
rich. The only other way of getting it
is to be born rich. If you have money,
that's power without having to be
powerful. I often think that it's all a big
conspiracy [and] that the winners are
the government and people like us
who've got the money. That joke about
keeping the workers ignorant is still
true; that's what they said about the
Tories and the landowners and that.
Then Labor were meant to educate the
workers, but they don't seem to be
doing that anymore."

March 25, 1966

LIVING IN A BOX

At the request of photographer Robert
Whitaker, the Beatles took part in a
series of highly experimental shots that
exploited their public image. The
group instantly warmed to Whitaker's
left-field approach and happily acquiesced to his often strange and at times
surreal demands in the studio. Aside
from sticking their heads through card-
board boxes and into a rusty birdcage,
the boys donned white coats and
adorned themselves with chunks of raw
meat and dismembered parts of children's dolls. The finished product,
known as the "Butcher Sleeve,"
remains the group's most controversial
photograph, with opinion veering
from "relevant" to "bad taste."

NME WINNERS

Dwarfed by a six-foot-six-inch Clint
Walker (star of *Cheyenne*, a popular
Western TV show), the boys mount the
stage to accept their award after their
final British concert. Once again, the
group topped the list of *New Musical
Express* recipients, and picked up the
award from the stage of London's
Wembley Arena. They played just four
numbers that afternoon, the last being
their new single, "Paperback Writer."

May 19, 1966

"PAPERBACK WRITER" AND "RAIN"
The Beatles booked Abbey Road's
cavernous Studio 1 for an intensive
day's filming of the video for their
new single "Paperback Writer" and its
B-side, "Rain." This versatile film format was in its infancy in 1966, and the
Beatles were naturally keen to be at
the forefront of the new technology.
They were tired of the trek to television studios to promote their latest
records, and video ensured that a single
performance could be broadcast anywhere with little effort.

May 19, 1966

"TAXMAN"

George leaning over his new Gibson
SG guitar during a break in filming at
Abbey Road studios. George had three
of his own compositions on *Revolver*,
the Beatles' latest album, "Taxman"
being the highlight. In this song, a
stinging diatribe on the hefty amount
of money the Beatles were handing
over to the government each year,
George—the most financially astute
of the quartet—fully expresses his
contempt for the system.

George: "'Taxman' was when I first
realized that even though we had
started earning money, we were actually giving most of it away in taxes. It
was and still is typical."

May 19, 1966

Over the course of three years the
Beatles had allowed the fringes of
their hairstyles to grow longer and
longer so that by 1966, their carefully
preened tresses were edging toward
their shoulders. This, coupled with
their attachment to darkly tinted sunglasses, led to yet another fashion
statement, eagerly leapt upon by the
rest of the world.

Ringo: "I doubt if we'll be changing
our hairstyles for a while. I think the
next stage will be when we go bald."

May 19, 1966

"HELLO, ED!"

The boys horse around prior to filming
an insert for the *Ed Sullivan Show*. The
show seemingly had an open-door pol-
icy for the Beatles to appear whenever
they wanted and, even if they couldn't
appear live, they could promote their
latest single via film. On this occasion
"Paperback Writer" was given an air-
ing. Historically, it was the group's
first hit not to deal with the trivialities
of love and relationships. The record-
buying public in Britain, however, was
not entirely convinced of its sentiments,
and despite some spirited promotion,
the record failed to shoot to the customary number-one position on its
first week of release.

May 19, 1966

A REVOLVER OUTTAKE

During a break in filming, the boys
pose for some photos for their new
album release, *Revolver*. Robert
Whitaker, one of the Beatles' favorite
photographers in the mid-1960s, was
charged with taking the photograph.
The front of the cover had already
gone through a few incarnations: A
swirling, kaleidoscopic photomontage
by Robert Freeman had been jetti-
soned in favor of a highly imaginative
pen, ink, and photo collage by their
friend from Hamburg, Klaus
Voormann. The back of the cover
needed a somewhat more conventional
image, and Whitaker's fit the bill.

TAKING A BREAK

While Ringo puts his feet up, Paul seems very much at ease with his bass guitar duties during the filming of the video for "Paperback Writer." Sonically, the single was a departure for the group, and it expanded the rather narrow definition of the three-minute pop single that had been in place up to that time.

Paul: "I arrived at Weybridge and told John I had this idea of trying to write off to a publisher to become a paperback writer, and I said, 'I think it should be written like a letter.' I took a bit of paper out and I said it should be something like, 'Dear Sir or Madam, as the case may be . . .' and I proceeded to write it just like a letter in front of him, occasionally rhyming it. . . . And then we went upstairs and put the melody to it. John and I sat down and finished it all up, but it was tilted towards me; the original idea was mine. I had no music, but it's just a little bluesy song, not a lot of melody. Then I had the idea to do the harmonies, and we arranged that in the studio."

May 19, 1966

"Rain" was the most complex song the
Beatles had released to date. A vivid
saunter through the newly psychedelicized brain of John, the track was a
clue to the direction that the Beatles
would take over the next few years.
For the first time ever, the final moments
of the song were recorded backward,
which dovetailed brilliantly with the
track's overt hallucinogenic theme.
This device was purely accidental, the
happy by-product of one of John's
drug experiments.

John: "I got home about five in the
morning, stoned out of me head. I
staggered up to me tape recorder and
put it on, but it came out backwards,
and I was in a trance in the earphones,
what is it, what is it? It's too much,
you know, and I really wanted the
whole song backwards almost, and that
was it. So we tagged it on the end. I
just happened to have the tape on the
wrong way, it just came out backwards,
it just blew me mind. The voice sounds
like an old Indian."

May 19, 1966

WHEN THE RAIN COMES . . .
The Beatles face the lights and cameras
for a full-on rendition of John's B-side,
"Rain." Normally, within the industry
at that time, the flip side of a disc was
left to showcase some ignominious
track to fill up the blank vinyl space.
With their strict attention to quality
control, the Beatles always insisted on a
track worthy enough to accommodate
its premier side. "Rain" was no exception, and it has remained a pivotal
creative moment in the Beatles' oeuvre.

May 19, 1966

THE PEACOCKS SPREAD THEIR FEATHERS

The boys take a breather between takes while recording video clips to accompany "Paperback Writer" and "Rain." Everything in the Beatles' wardrobe had changed in the space of a few months, and they were reveling in this new evolution. John in particular was taken with the new mood, branching out musically and otherwise in a multitude of directions. They were helped, in no small part, by their ingestion of LSD. Not exactly illegal in the mid-1960s, the drug had become a fashionable accoutrement of the swinging set around London, and the Beatles weren't shy about exploring the chemical's hallucinogenic landscapes for new sounds and dimensions that might inform their music.

Cynthia Lennon: "The peacock spread its fine feathers, dazzling colors and clothes took the place of conservative suits and ties."

May 20, 1966

ANOTHER FACE
George sitting quietly by himself at
London's Chiswick House between
takes. The Beatles had taken over the
grounds of this eighteenth-century
house to film some more promotional
slots for "Paperback Writer" and
"Rain" (though this time on celluloid).
George's profile had been raised considerably since recording three songs
for the group's imminent album
release, *Revolver.*

George: "I don't really know
whether I would've written more songs
by now, or better songs by now, had
Paul and John not been with us,
because probably I mightn't have even
thought of writing songs, only for
those two. But it was hard trying to
get in on it. . . . I've written so many
songs that I've just thrown away."

May 20, 1966

INSIDE THE CONSERVATORY OF CREATIVITY
The boys wait patiently as the next
sequence for "Paperback Writer" is set
up at Chiswick House. The boys'
natty gear was courtesy of the trendy
Chelsea boutique, Hung on You.
Previously the group had relied on the
somewhat conservative clothing skills
of showbiz tailor Dougie Millings.

May 20, 1966

RINGO TAKES THE AIR AT CHISWICK HOUSE
Since meeting with the American
folk-rock band, the Byrds, the previous
summer, the boys were rarely seen
without their sunglasses, their new
fashionable accessory during the summer of 1966.

May 20, 1966

JUST PAUL

Paul escapes the rigors of filming at
Chiswick House to attend to some
minor details in the boys' itinerary. As
nearby schools were midterm, the group
was rarely interrupted during the day
and completed two films under the
direction of Michael Lindsay-Hogg,
who was best known for his work on
the ultra-hip television show, *Ready,
Steady, Go!*

May 20, 1966

THE BIG MAN AND THE BASS MAN
Paul and Beatle aide Mal Evans check
guitar and lens during a brief interlude
at Chiswick House. Mal had been a
loyal attendant to the Beatles' needs
since the early days of the Cavern.
While Neil Aspinall was charged with
sorting out the labyrinth of demands
on the Beatles' time and itinerary, Mal
was more of a hands-on man and was
always at the group's side to facilitate
any immediate request the boys might
have. Sadly, this genial and jovial char-
acter who defied his size and deportment was shot, mistakenly, and killed
by police in America in mid-1970.

May 20, 1966

IMAGES FROM CHISWICK HOUSE

During this bright early summer's day,
the group meandered through the twist-
ing paths and arboretum surrounding the
West London estate to record what are
generally considered to be some of the
finest promotional films, in themselves a
blueprint for the pop video format. On
hand to record the cinematic activities
was Robert Whitaker, the group's official
photographer at the time and a trusted
member of their inner circle. Whitaker
would shoot some of his best material of
the band at Chiswick House.

CYCLIC REVOLVER

Paul spends a few moments at Chiswick House tramping down the greenery while waiting for the next shot to start. Paul would leap upon any chance to engage in acts of boyish behavior, and occasionally his trips on public transportation were in defiance of his celebrity status.

Paul: "I used to say to George Harrison, 'God, I'd like to go on a bus again.' George would say, 'Why would you want to do that?' His dad had been a bus driver and I think maybe George could not see the romance of traveling on a bus that I would. I always saw it as sitting upstairs, smoking a pipe like a poet. Sitting on the top of a bus composing things."

May 20, 1966

TOP OF THE POPS LIVE!

The Beatles' refusal to do many live television appearances caused something of a ripple of discontent in the U.K.'s pop-show offices. Holding out no real hope of the Beatles ever appearing on BBC's *Top of the Pops*, producer Johnnie Stewart nonetheless wrote to Brian Epstein to inquire if the group might appear on the show to promote its new single. Surprisingly, they accepted the offer and agreed to appear live—their first such TV appearance in more than a year. Furthermore, they were happy to play both sides of their new release. These images show the group in its natty gear during afternoon rehearsals and later during the performance itself.

June 16, 1966

RHYTHM KING

Ringo drums up a storm at the recording for the Beatles' last live BBC appearance on *Top of the Pops*. Ringo's drumming during 1966 reached a new level of ingenuity and subtlety, something that many had felt was beyond Ringo's steady but unremarkable skills as a "skin-pounder." On "Rain" in particular Ringo displayed a range of rhythms that elevated his status among his musical peers.

Ringo: "My favorite piece of me is what I did on 'Rain.' I think I just played amazing. I was into the snare and hi-hat. I think it was the first time I used the trick of starting a break by hitting the hi-hat first instead of going directly to a drum off the high hat. I think it's the best out of all the records I've ever made. 'Rain' blows me away. It's out in left field. I know me and I know my playing . . . and then there's 'Rain.'"

June 23, 1966

At Heathrow Airport, boarding flight
number BE 502 at 11:05 a.m. bound
for Munich, Germany. The boys' smiles
as they prepare to board the plane offer
no clue as to what had become for them
a living nightmare. Such was their dis-
satisfaction with playing live that they
hadn't even bothered to rehearse
material for their upcoming shows.
And with Japan, the Philippines, and
America waiting for them after the
German leg of their tour, it was going
to be a long, hot summer.

John: "We could send out four wax-
work dummies of ourselves and that
would satisfy the crowds. Beatles' concerts are nothing to do with music anymore. They're just bloody tribal rites."

GETTING BACK

Meeting the press at the Hotel
Bayerischer Hof in Munich. Seeing
as Germany had played a part in
nurturing the Beatles' early sound,
the band's arrival in the country was
especially affable. As had become the
norm, the group was presented with
a number of gifts, including four sets
of traditional German lederhosen.

Q: "What are you going to do with
your lederhosen?"

Paul: "I don't know. Probably hang
them up, eventually."

Q: "You're not going to wear them?"

Paul: "Oh, I might do, yeah. It's too
hot at the moment."

June 24, 1966

OH, WHAT A CIRCUS!
Onstage at Munich's Circus Krone-
Bau, the group's first concert in
Germany since December 1962. The
band was given a warm welcome, but
the quality of their sound was at such a
low that other musicians found their
performance disappointing.

Cliff Bennett (support artist in
Germany): "They'd actually given up
trying to play properly. . . . I think
they got sucked into the whole aura of
the thing. John went up there with a
very lax thing. It wasn't the band I saw
on the way up at the Star Club."

June 25, 1966

A specially chartered train had been
planned for the boys' tour of Germany,
and here they enjoy a few moments of
repose en route from Munich to Essen.
The train had been converted to accommodate Queen Elizabeth II on her trip
to the country the year before and consisted of four bedrooms, a bathroom,
and an expansive lounge.

Q: "There's an old German song that
says, 'Why is it so beautiful on the
Rhine?' You've traveled along the
Rhine, what are your impressions?"

John: "We were asleep!"

June 25, 1966

The boys gave a few perfunctory
glances in the direction of the press
aboard their specially chartered train
en route to Essen. The couple of press
conferences that were held in the country were hardly illuminating, although,
as always, the boys' comments proved
humorous.

Q: "If you would have to buy a ticket
for your own performance, how much
would you pay for it?"

John: "We know the manager, so we
get in free."

June 30, 1966

Of all the Beatles, George was most
vociferous about his opposition to
touring, and when quizzed about
their onstage appeal, he was typically
ambivalent about it. Indeed, on this
Far Eastern tour the group came to a
decision to knock off touring later
that year.

George: "We think very little at all.
You know . . . we just do it. And if the
time comes when we don't have an
audience, then we'll think then about
it. But now we don't think."

June 30, 1966

THE BEATLES HIT THE STAGE
Captured on videotape by Japan's
television network, NHK, the Beatles
shambled through the 30-minute
set of their first of five Budokan
concerts. Due to their poor performance and problems with their onstage
equipment, manager Brian Epstein
instructed the networks not to broadcast the show and gave them an option
on an additional performance. Given
their increasing disenchantment with
live appearances, the group hadn't
bothered to rehearse.

John: "We don't really bother about
what we do onstage anymore. We
practice what we call 'grinning at
nothings' . . . one-two-three-four,
and we all grin at nothing."

Even behind the Beatles' stage at the Budokan, security was in full force. For every concert, 3,000 police and army personnel mingled among the 10,000-capacity crowd. Death threats had been issued against the group for their alleged violation of the sacredness of the Budokan venue, which was normally used for sumo wrestling and other traditional Japanese sports. The demonstrations against the Beatles' performances there had stunned authorities, who were not used to seeing burning flags and violence in the streets from students. If any harm had come to the Beatles during their stay in Tokyo, it would have sparked an enormous diplomatic crisis.

George: "It was strange because there had been students rioting against the cops and it was like being back in World War II, because the police had those little steel helmets I remember we used to have leftover from the war."

June 30, 1966

INSIDE THE BUDOKAN ARENA
More than 210,000 ticket applications
had been received for just 30,000
available seats for the original three
Tokyo shows. Given the enormous
clamor for tickets, two matinee shows
were added to the itinerary. Security
had never been tighter for a Beatles
concert. Plainclothes officers with
telephoto lenses photographed any
audience member who attempted to
breach the tight security.

Paul: "The thing is, if the security is
strict then it is probably best for us and
the people as well. Sometimes it's too
strict, but the best situation is when
it's just strict enough so that nobody
gets hurt."

July 2, 1966

The boys climb the imposing staircase
to the stage at the Budokan Arena for a
matinee performance.

Alf Bicknell (Beatles driver): "The
strange thing about this was if you
looked between the rows of seats there
were stewards and ushers, and every
time a Japanese Beatles fan would jump
up, they were quickly, but gently, put
back into their seats."

July 2, 1966

EMPEROR'S NEW CLOTHES
Relaxed but bored, John smokes in
his kimono as the hours pass slowly
between shows in the Beatles' Tokyo
hotel suite.

John: "When I look as though I am
having fun, I am, you know. When
I'm not, I'm not. So it varies."

July 2, 1966

AMONG THE PRESENTS
George, Ringo, and John review yet
another batch of gifts sent up to their
presidential suite. The Tokyo police
informed the Beatles that for security
reasons they were never to leave the
confines of their suite, other than to
go to the Budokan for their concerts.
So instead of seeing Tokyo, Tokyo was
brought to them. Upset by what they
felt to be totally unnecessary precau-
tions, the Beatles just lazed around
dressed in ceremonial kimonos, as
company representatives paraded a
succession of trinkets and gadgets
before them.

TRADITIONAL SOUNDS

George adopts a traditional tea-drink-
ing stance while Ringo plucks one of
a seeming endless succession of gifts
brought up to the Beatles' Tokyo
Hilton suite. The Beatles, especially
George, were by this time immersing
themselves fully in the new sounds
from overseas. A couple of years previously, this instrument would have been
treated as little more than a curiosity.
By 1966, in the spirit of the experimental direction the Beatles' were now
moving into, new instruments were
eagerly explored.

July 2, 1966

DIFFERENT SHADES

John and George shoot the breeze in their Tokyo suite. Even though the group spent just short of one hundred hours on Japanese soil the boys saw little, if anything, of the country.

John: "We're not on holiday. We don't expect to see any sights or have any fun. And if we get fun as well while we happen to be touring, well then it's okay, you know. But it's our job as well."

July 2, 1966

WITHIN WITHOUT YOU
George relaxing at the Tokyo Hilton
between shows. It was George who
had become the most disillusioned
with the chaos attached to the group's
touring caravan and was the principal
catalyst for the group's decision to quit
performing later that year.

July 2, 1966

To idle away the long hours they spent
in their hotel suite, the Beatles played
little music, preferring instead to tinker
with their new electronic gadgets,
drink sake, and smoke marijuana. After
their shows at the Budokan, the group
worked on a collage, their only collaborative work of art.

Robert Whitaker (Beatles photographer): "I never saw them calmer, more
contented, than at this time. They were
working on something that let their
personalities come out. I think it's the
only work they ever did together that
has nothing to do with music. They'd
stop, go and do a concert, and then it
was, 'Let's get back to the picture.'"

July 2, 1966

PICTURE YOURSELF

John getting into his side of the canvas.
The finished piece, entitled *Four Images
of a Woman*, was presented to the president of their Japanese fan club as a gift.
In 2002 it was offered for sale on an
Internet auction site with an asking
price of $250,000.

July 8, 1966

BACK HOME

The relief is palpable as the boys arrive
back at Heathrow after a tour that had
included a brief stint in the Philippines.
While in Manila, the group had unin-
tentionally upset the president's wife,
Imelda Marcos, by failing to turn up
for a reception she'd organized in their
honor. This perceived snub created a
national furor that resulted in the
withdrawal of security and assistance
for their safe passage out of the country. On attempting to fly out, they
were met by a crowd of supporters
loyal to the presidency who were bent
on confronting the group for its apparent indignities against the Marcoses. In
the chaos that ensued, several of the
Beatles' touring contingent were injured
as the group ran across the tarmac
toward its plane.

SPILLING THE BEANS

Four very weary Beatles made their customary trip to Heathrow's press-room to impart the exact details of their horrendous Philippines trip. The Beatles were adamant that after the treatment they received from certain individuals and security personnel, they would never set foot in the country again.

Paul: "We got to the airport and our road managers had a lot of trouble trying to get the equipment in because the escalators had been turned off. So we got there, and we got put into the transit lounge. And we got pushed around from one corner of the lounge to another."

John: "We'll just never go to any nut-houses again."

"WE'RE MORE POPULAR THAN JESUS"
John relaxes on the 27th floor of the Astor Towers Hotel in Chicago after facing the American press for the first time since his "We're more popular than Jesus" furor. Any notion that the Beatles were in for an easy spell after the controversy surrounding their Japan and Philippines concerts was dashed when a months-old quote that John had made to journalist Maureen Cleave was taken out of context and recycled onto the front of American teen magazine, *Datebook*. Prior to the tour, the Beatles had got wind that certain sections of the U.S. were incandescent with rage at John's comment and were holding carefully staged bonfires to dispose of what they saw as the blasphemous ephemera of Beatlemania. Many publicity-conscious radio stations in the Deep South were complicit in the brouhaha against the group; it was they who whipped the controversy into a frenzy, conveniently in time for the group's arrival in Chicago on August 11. John, never censured for his bold views, was upset at the outrage and, against his better judgment, made what appeared to be an apology to the assembled news media. On closer inspection, however, his words that day were more a reiteration of his initial observations on the decline of Christianity.

John: "I was pointing it out. I mean, if somebody like us says it, people sort of do take notice, you know, even church people are trying to be 'with it' with pop groups and things. They're still doing it the wrong way, and I was just stating a fact as I saw it. And I wasn't trying to compare me or the group with Jesus or religion at all."

August 20, 1966

GLASSES ON, HEADS DOWN
Aboard a chartered Greyhound bus,
the Beatles make a somber approach to
Busch Stadium in St. Louis, Missouri.
Predictably, John's "Jesus" comment
hit hardest in the South, but despite
considerable pressure to cancel the
shows there, the group went ahead
with its performances.

Q: "What is your feeling about going
down South where most of this controversy has arisen?"

John: "Well, I hope that if we sort
of try and talk to the press and people
and that, you know, you can judge
for yourselves what it meant, I think,
better by seeing us."

ONE MORE TIME

The Beatles were afforded a rare
luxury—a day off between concerts
on their last jaunt around the States. To
satisfy the East Coast contingent of
media, a couple of press conferences
were slotted into their resting hours at
the Warwick Hotel in New York. The
sessions themselves were still heavily
dominated by the religious controversy
and the dwindling concert attendance.

Q: "There appear to be a much smaller
number of fans outside the hotel, and
the concert tomorrow night at Shea
Stadium is far below a sellout. How do
you feel about this?"

John: "Very rich."

August 22, 1966

ON THE WANE?
Shea Stadium, New York. Although
more than 40,000 fans were present
for the Beatles' second concert at Shea,
more than 11,000 of the cheaper seats
had failed to sell. Seven days later, at
a three-quarter full Candlestick Park
in San Francisco, it was all over; the
Beatles' live career had drawn to a close.

Fan at Shea Stadium: "They have
everything: talent and good looks and
the English accents everybody looks
for. The Beatles are the greatest guys
that ever existed."

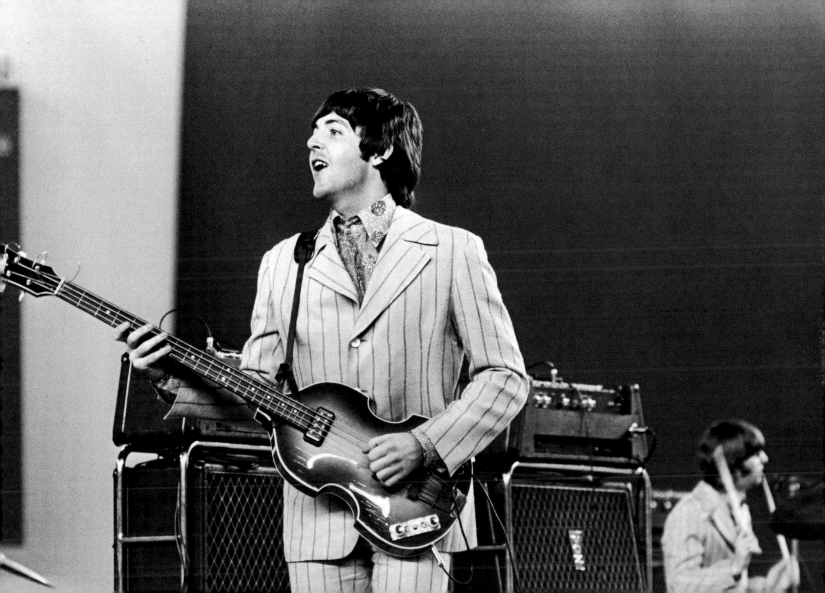

September 5, 1966

Flanked by Beatles assistant Alistair
Taylor, John climbs out of his car at
Heathrow where he'll catch a flight to
Germany for his solo film debut. Now
that the Beatles' troubled touring
schedule had finally ground to a halt,
the boys were keen to pursue other
avenues. Finding much to identify with
in the script, John accepted an offer
from film director Richard Lester to
appear in a major role in his new film
How I Won the War.

John: "I feel I want to be them all—
painter, writer, actor, singer, player,
musician. I want to try them all, and
I'm lucky enough to be able to. I want
to see which one turns me on. This is
for me, this film, because apart from
wanting to do it because of what it
stands for, I want to see what I'll be
like when I've done it."

September 8, 1966

WAITING FOR THE NEXT SHOT?
Relaxing in a field in Celle, Germany.
To look the part for *How I Won the
War,* John had to have his locks paired
back to befit a 1940s conscript—an
act deemed so outrageous in 1966 that
the world's press converged at the
location to witness the sacrilegious act
of a Beatle cutting his hair. Although
he looks pretty composed in this shot,
John was, in fact, dreading his first
project outside the Beatles.

John: "I was just a bundle of nerves
the first day. I couldn't hardly speak I
was so nervous. My first speech was
in a forest, on patrol. I was supposed
to say, 'My heart's not in it anymore,'
and it wasn't. I went home and said to
myself, 'Either you're not going to be
like that, or you're going to give up.'"

September 8, 1966

CONSCIENTIOUS AND OBJECTIVE
Among the desert sands, John got to
grips with an assortment of military
weapons that were integral to his role
of Musketeer Gripweed. Although
he was still exploring his own inert
pacifism, he was keen to elaborate on
an anti-war stance when interviewed
during filming.

John: "If they said, 'Fight the war
now,' my age group would fight the
war. Not that they'd want to. There
might be a bit more trouble getting
them in line, because I'd be up there
shouting, 'Don't do it!'"

MELODY MAKERS

With George vacationing in India and
John filming in Spain, there was still
Beatles business to attend to in London.
Paul and Ringo, enjoying the first significant break from their hectic
schedule in months, were on hand to
receive awards from *Melody Maker*
magazine in the exclusive restaurant
atop London's Post Office Tower.
Making the presentations that day were
American crooner Johnny Mathis,
while Tom Jones and Dusty Springfield
also picked up some awards. Paul and
Ringo made the required gestures to
the press before moving off to resume
their break.

IT'S NOT UNUSUAL
Paul, Dusty Springfield, Tom Jones,
and Ringo at the *Melody Maker* awards.
Toward the end of 1966 (often noted
as the halfway point in their career),
the Beatles would stop attending award
ceremonies, having become exhausted
by the superficiality of such gatherings.

Early October 1966

GOLDEN SANDS AND STRAWBERRY FIELDS
Filming continues in the desert. Since
How I Won the War was shot principally
on location in Almeria, Spain, the production unit kept traveling distances to
a minimum. John spent more than nine
weeks in the Spanish province and
although he had wife Cynthia and
Beatle aide Neil Aspinall in tow, he
called on additional companionship
from Ringo, who came out for a number of days during shooting.

The interminable waiting, not unusual during a film shoot, was a highly
productive time for John, and the spar-
tan living accommodations did nothing
to detract from John's composing one
of his greatest songs, "Strawberry
Fields Forever."

John: "It did me a lot of good to get
away. . . . I wrote 'Strawberry Fields
Forever' there. It gave me time to think
on my own, away from the others.
From then on, I was looking for somewhere to go, but I didn't have the nerve
to really step out on the boat by myself
and push it off."

October 26, 1966

During his holiday in India, George had lodged with sitar maestro Ravi Shankar for lessons on the complex and highly idiosyncratic instrument. George returned the favor when Shankar paid a trip to the U.K. a few weeks later; the now fully Easternized Beatle was on hand to chauffeur the musician to his home in Esher, Surrey.

Ravi Shankar: "[George] is an enthusiastic and ambitious student because he realizes that the sitar itself is an 'envolvement' (sic) from Indian culture. It might take a lifetime of learning, but if he progresses in the same way that he has been doing, his understanding will lead to a medium of greatness on the sitar."

November 24, 1966

DIFFERENT DIRECTIONS

George and Ringo arrive at EMI Recording Studios to join the other Beatles to begin recording after a five-month break; "Strawberry Fields Forever" is the result of this night's session. The gamut of influences picked up in their time off helped turn the Beatles' sound and image in new directions. Gone were the monochrome tailoring and single-dimensional sounds; the accent was now on experimentation and consciousness expansion. Although this was a delight to many of their admirers, the decision to abandon live performances for the solitude of the studio created speculation in certain quarters that the group was close to splitting up.

Paul: "If we're not listened to, and we can't even hear ourselves, we can't get any better. So we're trying to get better with things like recording."

John: "We're always involved with each other whatever we're doing, you know . . . we'll probably carry on writing music forever, you know, whatever else we're doing. You just can't stop. You find yourself doing it whether you want to or not."

George: "Everything we've done so far has been rubbish as far as I see it today. It doesn't mean a thing to what we want to do now."

November 24, 1966

YES? WHAT?
Ringo and George give a slightly jaun-
diced glance at the camera before
starting work at EMI's Abbey Road
studios. Ringo, an integral part of the
band's unit, was yet to find his own
niche outside of the Beatles' frame.

Ringo: "I'm sort of out of it there
because, with John and Paul, they can
still write even though we're sort of
not working together. And George
can, you know, learn his sitar and do
things like that. And I've just been sitting around."

November 27, 1966

MAKING A SPECTACLE

During the Beatles' hiatus from touring, John had fully ingratiated himself
in the dinner-party circles of London's
celebrity set. One personality John
befriended was satirical comedian Peter
Cook. John had already appeared in a
cameo on Cook and Dudley Moore's
television show *Not Only . . . But Also*
in 1965 and was again called upon, this
time to participate in a humorous skit
outside a men's public bathroom in
London's Soho. John was pitched as a
commissioner against Cook's role as an
American television producer in search
of swinging London. The irony of a
celebrity toilet was certainly not lost
on John.

John: "There's more talk about it
than is actually happening. You know,
swinging this, and all that. Everybody
can go around in England with long
hair a bit, and boys can wear flowered
trousers and flowered shirts and things
like that, but there's still the same old
nonsense going on. It's just that we're
all dressed up a bit different."

January 8, 1967

BLUES BROTHERS

Keyboard supremo Georgie Fame
drives a friendly wedge between John
and Paul at Kensington's trendy night-
club the Cromwellian ("3 floors of fun
in Kensington"). The fancy-dress event
was held to celebrate the 21st birthday
of Fame's fiancee, Carmen Jimenez,
and a sizable contingent of London's
beautiful people were on the guest list.
Fame would play a key role in Paul's
destiny: A gig of his held in May 1967
would draw the Beatle together with
one Linda Eastman.

Linda Eastman: "Paul was there
with a bunch of friends at the table
next to us and it was one of those
things . . . just giving each other the
eye, we just fancied each other."

February 10, 1967

A DAY IN THE LIFE

Abbey Road's Studio 1 recording session for the orchestral augmentation to "A Day in the Life." The track, perhaps the finest example of the Lennon/McCartney collaborative partnership, was earmarked as the coda to their most ambitious project to date: *Sgt. Pepper's Lonely Hearts Club Band*. To pad-out the last 24 bars of dead air following the end of the song, the group put it to producer George Martin that they wanted an orchestration that would be the equivalent of a musical "orgasm." Thus, 40 classically trained musicians entered EMI's studios on the evening of February 10 to begin painstakingly laying down an ascending montage of sound building to a crescendo before a crashing major E took the piece out to silence. The Beatles now had a truly majestic ending to one of their finest works.

John: "We thought we wanted a growing noise to lead back into the first bit. We wanted to think of a good end and we had to decide what sort of backing and instruments would sound good. Like all our songs, they never become an entity until the very end. They are developed all the time as we go along."

February 10, 1967

CATCHING THE LIGHT
Ringo filming a scarf waved by John
during the "Day in the Life" session.
With them is film director Peter
Goldman.

Not content with the fusion of the
classical and avant-garde spheres on
Sgt. Pepper, the Beatles were prepared
to step out even further and produce a
film to accompany their new collection. Now an acceptable by-product of
any new album release, the project was
conceived to add color to their already
multihued musical offering. In the
end, the project floundered, but the
specially shot film from the evening
of February 10 still exists and is as
chaotic and joyously fragmented as
the evening's events.

April 12, 1967

A MAGICAL MYSTERY

Paul arrives back at Heathrow after an
eight-day holiday in the States. The
break was ostensibly to be with girlfriend Jane Asher on her 21st birthday
in Denver, Colorado, where she was
performing in repertory. However,
during his Stateside visit Paul would
take off in various directions along the
West Coast, visiting Jefferson Airplane
in Haight Ashbury and recording with
the Beach Boys during sessions for
their controversial album, *Smile*. It
was during this brief sojourn into the
hinterlands of California hippydom
that Paul, feeding off the residual ener-
gy left by Ken Kesey's band of psychedelic travelers, would form ideas that
would later see light in the group's
project *Magical Mystery Tour*.

Paul: "I really wish the people that
look at the 'weirdos,' at the 'happen-
ings,' at the psychedelic 'freak-outs,'
would, instead of just looking with
anger, just look with nothing; with
no feeling; be unbiased about it."

April 29, 1967

EVER THE GENTLEMAN
Paul greets Jane Asher off the plane
after her theater tour of the States.
Asher had been performing with the
Bristol Old Vic repertory company.
Word had it that on her return to
London, the red-headed starlet was
far from impressed with the newly
psychedelicized Paul.

Paul: "This [LSD] opened my eyes to
the fact there is a God . . . I had never
realized what people were talking about
when they said God is within you."

May 18, 1967

A WALK IN THE PARK
America was slowly catching on to
the fact that the changes happening
within the Beatles went deeper than
the lovable mop-top image. Certainly,
their current look was in stark contrast to that portrayed in the cartoon
series being broadcast across the States
(which the Beatles detested). The
weekly journal, *Life*, dispatched a team
of researchers over to London to find
out what was driving the Beatles' new
creative streak, and arranged for several interviews and photo sessions, one of
which was in Hyde Park. The reporters
got more than they bargained for, and
questions to Paul about psychedelics
revealed an almost evangelic admiration for LSD.

Paul: "God is the space between us.
God is on the table in front of you.
It just happens I realize all this
through acid."

May 19, 1967

ELITE PERSONNEL

To usher in the Beatles' new master-piece, *Sgt. Pepper's Lonely Hearts Club Band*, Brian Epstein hosted a small soiree for an elite retinue of media per-sonnel at his plush home in London's Belgravia. The Beatles, fully decked out in their current hippy regalia, were a bit worse for wear due to the ingestion of some illicit substances prior to the gathering, although they happily posed for the photographers, one of whom was a young American called Linda Eastman. If anything, it was the transformation of John that shocked many of those present that evening. Evidently, the lifestyle he was adopting was taking a considerable toll on him.

Ray Coleman (journalist): "John looked haggard, old, ill, and hopelessly addicted to drugs. His eyes were glazed, his speech slow and slurred."

May 19, 1967

INSIDER DELIGHTS

After having become increasingly skeptical about the objectives of the press,
the Beatles were nonetheless happy
to promote their album *Sgt. Pepper's
Lonely Hearts Club Band*. Adding to the
delights on offer, the group ensured
that the packaging was as eye-catching
and as compelling as the album it
housed.

Paul: "We realized for the first time
that someday someone would actually
be holding a thing that they'd call 'the
Beatles' new LP' and that normally it
would just be a collection of songs or a
nice picture on the cover, nothing more.
So the idea was to do a complete thing
that you could make what you liked
of—just a little magic presentation. We
were going to have a little envelope in
the center with the nutty things you can
buy at Woolworth's: a surprise packet."

May 19, 1967

Although Paul and Linda had already
met at a Georgie Fame gig four days
earlier, this was the first time they were
photographed together. Linda, a noted
photographer in the States, had come
over to England with the intention of
capturing images of the burgeoning
British psychedelic scene. Naturally,
high on her list was a chance to secure
an audience with the Beatles. As luck
would have it, the *Sgt. Pepper* press
conference coincided with her trip, and
after a meeting with Brian Epstein's
assistant, Peter Brown, she was offered
a highly prized invite to the gathering.

Peter Brown: "Linda sank to her
knees in front of his chair and began
snapping photos of him. Although she
tried to manage otherwise, she left
with all the other photographers."

May 19, 1967

VICTORIAN WATCHMAKER
The Beatles' sartorial choice at the
Sgt. Pepper gathering was as way-out
as their sounds playing in the background. As this was their first official
press gathering since fully expanding
into psychedelia, the press was keen to
note every detail of their new apparel.

Melody Maker: "Lennon won the
sartorial stakes with a green flower-
patterned shirt, red cord trousers,
yellow socks, and what looked like
cord shoes. His ensemble was completed by a sporran. With his bushy
side-boards and National Health specs,
he resembled a Victorian watchmaker.
Paul McCartney, sans moustache,
wore a loosely tied scarf over a shirt,
a striped double-breasted jacket, and
looked like something out of a Scott
Fitzgerald novel."

May 25, 1967

PSYCHEDELIC LIVERY

In the whirlwind of the psychedelic
revolution, vivid color and seamless
patterns were the order of the moment.
George had recently painted his
bungalow in Day-Glo colors, and in
keeping with the flavor of the times,
John's Rolls Royce underwent the
psychedelic paintbrush for the princely
sum of a thousand pounds. Although
now totally unrecognizable as the vehicle that drove the boys to Buckingham
Palace for their MBE investiture in
1965, it nonetheless drew a huge crowd
on its unveiling in Chertsey, Surrey,
after a six-week renovation by a local
bus company. The press, ever skeptical
about the Beatles' metamorphosis from
cheeky mop-tops to full-blown hippies,
were less than impressed.

The Sun: "It looks like a public
raspberry being blown loudly and
continuously by the young and famous
owner of a lot of money."

FACING THE MUSIC

On the steps facing his garden at 7 Cavendish Avenue, in London's St. John's Wood, Paul holds two newborn kittens while faithful companion Martha looks on. It was quite an eventful day for the Beatle, symbolic in a sense, as this was the day he finally lost the "divinity" he'd long held with the press. Paul's admission to *Life* magazine that he had experimented with the "heaven-and-hell drug," LSD, was seized upon by the world's media. With their way-out clothes and experimental music, it was by now patently obvious where the Beatles' inspirations were coming from. Paul would be vilified for his LSD comments, and by association, the other Beatles would be heavily implicated (much to their intense annoyance). During this day, a news team from television station ITN turned up at Paul's house demanding an interview regarding the scandal, and Paul, without consulting Brian Epstein or any of the other Beatles, innocently agreed to the request.

Q: "Do you think that you have now encouraged your fans to take drugs?"

Paul: "I don't think it'll make any difference. I don't think my fans are going to take drugs just because I did, you know? But the thing is, that's not the point, anyway. I was asked whether I had or not. And from then on, the whole bit about how far it's going to go and how many people it's going to encourage is up to the newspapers, and up to you on television. I mean, you're spreading this now, at this moment. This is going into all the homes in Britain. And I'd rather it didn't. But you're asking me the question, you want me to be honest, I'll be honest."

Q: "But as a public figure, surely you've got the responsibility to . . ."

Paul: "No, it's *you* who've got the responsibility. You've got the responsibility not to spread this now. You know, I'm quite prepared to keep it as a very personal thing if you will, too. If you'll shut up about it, I will."

June 21, 1967

PREPARING TO ENCHANT

The Beatles arrive at EMI studios to
begin work on their next single. Under
normal circumstances, this would have
been just another day at the studio,
but this was to be yet another milestone in their career. The Beatles had
been selected to act as Britain's representatives in *Our World*, the first simul-
taneous live world-television broadcast,
and, in retrospect, the first display of
the "global village" concept. Typically
nonplussed by the enormity of the
event, the group left the recording of
its contribution to the show, "All You
Need Is Love," to a few days prior to
the actual broadcast. Poignantly, the
taping of this track would be the last
time Brian Epstein would attend a
Beatles recording session.

Brian Epstein: "It is a wonderful,
beautiful, spine-chilling record. It cannot be misinterpreted. It is a clear
message saying that love is everything.
It is the best thing they've done."

June 21, 1967

THERE'S NOTHING YOU CAN SING . . .
Paul enters the doors of Abbey Road
studios to put down the backing track
to "All You Need Is Love." Years later,
Paul would rate the song and its
recording session as one of the high-
points of the band's career.

Paul: "It was a way of putting this
philosophy to everyone, and it was an
exciting evening anyway because we'd
worked on it for a few days, rehearsing
it and knowing what we were going to
do, and then we piled all our friends
into the studio, which was great."

June 21, 1967

I WANT TO TELL YOU
George waltzes into Abbey Road studios to begin work on "All You Need Is
Love." As the Beatle who was most
enamored of the love-generation philosophy, the song was much in keeping
with George's thinking at the time.

George: "The hippies are a good idea.
I love all these people . . . the ones
who are honest and trying to find a
bit of truth, and to straighten out the
untruths. I'm with them one hundred
percent."

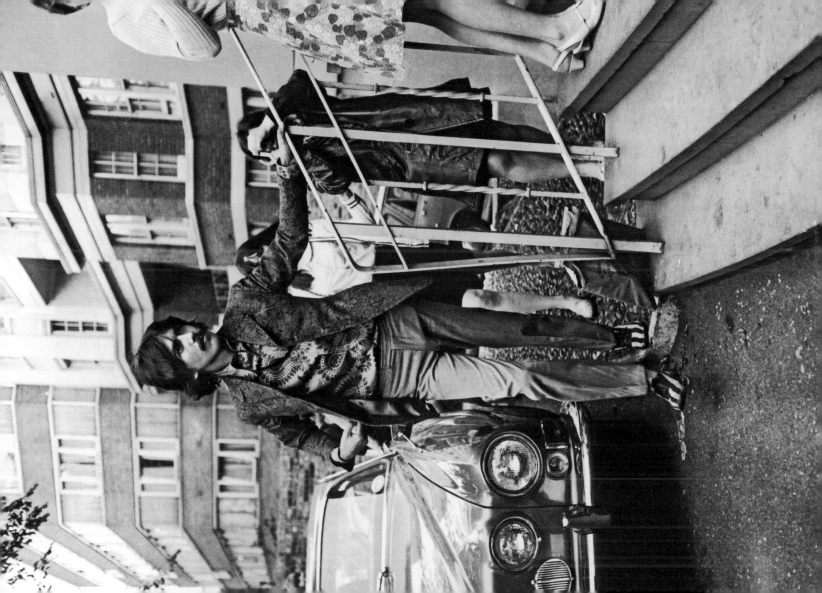

June 24, 1967

READY TO SING TO THE WORLD

To give Fleet Street's finest the opportunity to have their pictures developed
and in the morning papers, EMI
invited a huge posse of journalists and
photographers into Abbey Road's
cavernous Studio 1 for an audience
with the Beatles prior to their world
satellite broadcast. With the title "All
You Need Is Love" now fully installed
in the public's awareness, the Beatles
were more than happy to use the occasion to promote the message of the
song—a sentiment that was finding
favor with youth around the world.

Paul: "We had been told we'd be seen
recording it by the whole world at the
same time. So we had one message for
the world—love. We need more love
in the world."

June 24, 1967

The Beatles spent a considerable amount of time posing for photographers and answering questions from the press during the media reception to launch their new single. "All You Need Is Love" was warmly received by the media, who were perhaps a little relieved that the Beatles' current penchant for experimentation hadn't dulled their hit-making potential.

Daily Mirror: "Like old soldiers returning from the front with flowers in their berets, the Beatles are battling back again after much criticism."

June 24, 1967

Perhaps the least disposed of the four
to press gatherings, George nonetheless
put on a display of conviviality at
EMI's studios, and happily espoused
his beliefs.

George: "The thing is, everybody is
potentially divine. It's just a matter of
self-realization before it will all happen.
The whole point of life is to harmonize
with everything and every aspect of
creation."

June 29, 1967

PRIVATE BEATLE

Although intensely guarded when it
came to his family's privacy, John con-
sented to a rare glimpse of himself and
son Julian at home and was happy to
show a trusted photographer around
the Surrey-based manor and its expansive grounds. John was never truly
happy about the property and privately
confided that he despised its bourgeois
atmosphere, although its location offered
some much-needed distance from
swinging London's 24-hour madness.

SUBURBAN SPLENDOR

The mock Tudor splendor of Kenwood, home to John, Cynthia, and son Julian from the end of July 1964 until early 1969.

John bought the St. George's Hill property for £20,000 after a tip from Beatles accountant Walter Strach, who was a resident of nearby Weybridge. Before moving into the house, John ordered considerable renovations both inside and out, and with a brief to design something modern but unique, designer Kenneth Partridge transformed the 27-room house into a palace fit for a Beatle.

The property was adjacent to a golf course, and initially the stuffy guardians of the establishment were concerned about the possible hordes of rampant Beatlemaniacs clambering over their precious turf for a glimpse of the reclusive Beatle. In an act of preventative defiance, the club issued a statement saying that neither John nor Ringo, another Weybridge resident, would be welcome as members of the club (not that it bothered either Beatle).

John: "I nearly didn't buy the house when I heard there was a course at the back of it, because I had fears of people running all over my garden looking for their golf balls. We haven't asked to become members of the club and we won't be doing so. Neither of us has the slightest interest in the sport."

CARAVAN OF LOVE

John ordered that the dainty caravan he'd bought for son Julian's fourth birthday should undergo a wash of psychedelia not dissimilar to the paint job on his Rolls. With John's Weybridge garden now resembling a gypsy fairground, the caravan at least seemed more at home under the rainbow swirls than his car (although complaints regarding both vehicles were raised by the local residents' association). When John had packed his bags and left this Surrey home in 1969, the caravan was airlifted to Dornish, an island off the west coast of Ireland, and has not been heard from since.

GREECE LIGHTNING

An almost unrecognizable John larks around on a hillside near Athens, Greece. The Beatles had repaired to the Greek islands for a short holiday toward the end of July 1967. Aside from the glorious weather virtually guaranteed in the Aegean, the group was keen to realize a combined utopian vision for an exclusive commune on an isolated island. At the time they did buy a sizable piece of land at considerable expense, but quickly lost interest in the concept of a shared Beatle paradise.

Brian Epstein: "I think it's a dotty idea, but they're no longer children and must have their own sweet way."

Mid-August, 1967

HOME ALONE
This and other family photos of the
Starrs at home offer a rare glimpse of
their life during the mid-1960s. Replete
with bar, pool room, go-cart track,
and cinema, Ringo's home, Sunny
Heights, was situated in the same
exclusive neighborhood as John's in
Weybridge, Surrey. Ringo had bought
the house in July 1965. George's home
was just a few miles away in Esher.

Ringo: "I'm the laziest Beatle. I'm
quite happy to finish an album and go
sit back. I can enjoy myself just sitting
back and playing with all the toys and
the kids and the wife. I enjoy playing
with the wife!"

August 24, 1967

RINGO WITH NEWBORN BABY JASON

A delighted Ringo at London's Queen
Charlotte Maternity Hospital where his
wife, Maureen, had just given birth to
their second son, soon to be christened
Jason. Ringo's paternal duties would
prevent him from joining his fellow
Beatles at a gathering in London's West
End that evening. The happening that
night featured the "next big thing" in
the group's ever continuing search
for meaning: its first meeting with
Maharishi Mahesh Yogi.

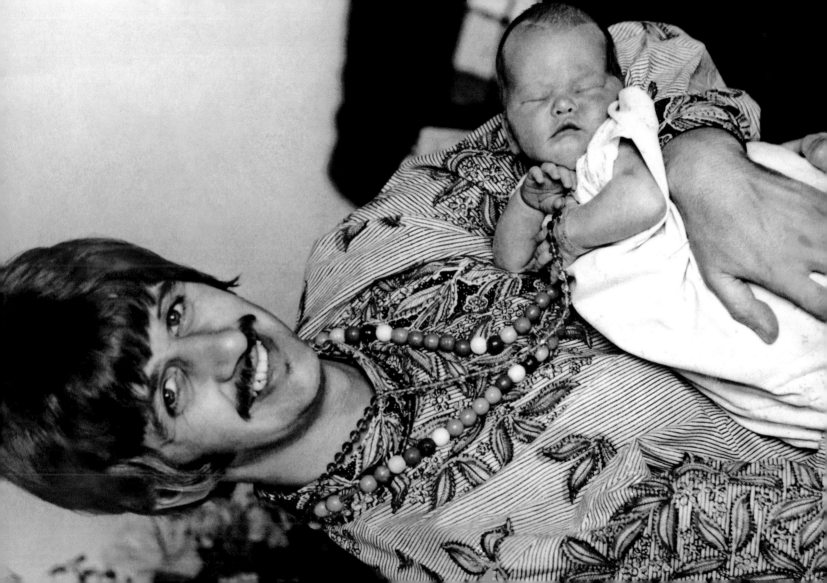

DIDN'T WE HAVE A LOVELY TIME THE DAY WE WENT TO BANGOR?

All four Beatles, their partners, plus Mick Jagger and girlfriend Marianne Faithfull arrive at Euston station in North London for another chapter in the Beatles' remarkable story. The previous night, George, accompanied by John, Paul, and their respective partners, had attended a presentation on meditation given by the Indian mystic, Maharishi Mahesh Yogi, at London's Hilton Hotel. The effect was immediate, and after an audience with the giggling guru, the group accepted the swami's invitation to join him for a weekend seminar in Bangor, North Wales, to become fully inducted into his gentle, mind-expanding process of transcendental meditation.

John: "Well, he was just doing a lecture in London at the Hilton. So we all went and we thought, 'What a nice man.' And we were looking for that. You know, everybody's looking for it, but we were looking for it that day as well. And then we met him and he was good, you know. He's got a good thing in him. And we went along with it."

August 25, 1967

BETTER LATE

Arriving late at Euston station after a
traffic holdup, John rushes to catch the
train for Bangor, North Wales, where
he will confer with the Maharishi
Mahesh Yogi.

John: "Maharishi was a father figure,
Elvis Presley might have been a father
figure. I don't know. Robert Mitchum.
Any male image is a father figure.
There's nothing wrong with it until
you give them the right to give you
sort of a recipe for your life."

August 25, 1967

A tearful Cynthia Lennon flanked by road manager Neil Aspinall, press officer Tony Barrow, and Brian Epstein's assistant, Peter Brown. The Beatles and their entourage arrived at the North London station with just seconds to spare to catch their train (which the press had dubbed the "Bangor Express"). In the rush, John's wife Cynthia was prevented from joining the Beatles' car by an overzealous policeman, who mistook her for a fan. Although Cynthia would later be driven to the Welsh venue to meet the party, this episode would come to represent the beginning of the end of her relationship with John. Although meditation had brought them closer together ideologically—Cynthia was an ardent opponent of his use of drugs—they were slowly drifting apart.

Cynthia Lennon: "I knew when I missed that train it was synonymous with all my premonitions for the future. I just knew in my heart, as I watched all the people that I loved fading away into the hazy distance, that *that* was to be my future."

INNER SANCTUM OF MYSTICISM
The Beatles with the maharishi at Normal College in Bangor, North Wales. The celebrity attached to the Beatles ensured that private audiences were de rigueur whenever they graced an occasion. On this night, the group met privately with the mystic after an evening lecture at the college. Despite his humble Eastern persona, the guru was aware of the immense global value that the Beatles' attentions had on his campaign and was keen to be photographed with them whenever possible. One positive and immediate effect that meditation had on the Beatles was to divert them away from drug use. The group was more than happy to publicly announce its abstinence from substances, which conveniently helped to redress the growing resentment toward the band over the drug issue.

Paul: "Now it's over. We don't need it anymore. We think we're finding new ways of getting there."

Ringo: "I've not taken any drugs since we've started on this meditation. I hope I will get so much out of this, I will not have to go back on drugs."

John: "If we'd met maharishi before we'd taken LSD, we wouldn't have needed to take it."

George: "LSD isn't a real answer. It doesn't give you anything. It enables you to see a lot of possibilities that you may never have noticed before, but it isn't the answer."

SHOCKED AND STUNNED

While retreating with the maharishi in Wales, the news filtered through to the Beatles' party that their friend and manager, Brian Epstein, had died in a drug-related death in his home in London. Shocked, Paul and Jane Asher left almost immediately to drive back to London, while a dazed George, John, and Ringo briefly hung around to share their immediate thoughts with the press. The news that Brian had died just as the group was finding its individuality without his guidance seems strangely prophetic.

John: "We don't know what to say. We loved him and he was one of us."

George: "You can't pay tribute in words."

Paul: "This is a great shock. I am terribly upset."

Ringo: "We loved Brian. He was a generous man. We owe so much to him."

ALONE AND TOGETHER

With Brian Epstein's death, the Beatles were alone (managerially, at least) for the first time in five years. Just a few days after their manager's untimely passing, Paul—ever the workhorse of the group—unveiled his ambitious yet wholly nebulous plans for *Magical Mystery Tour*, the Beatles first self-directed, self-produced film project. The idea was conceived to fill the vacuum left by Epstein's departure. The freewheeling concept of chartering a bus and loading it with actors, aging music-hall odd balls, and psychedelic eccentrics, all without a script or any direction, found tacit resistance from the other Beatles who were eager to keep the Beatles' show rolling.

Eschewing the complexities of filming, Paul undertook the majority of preproduction himself—a considerable task—and just ten days after the meeting to discuss the project, they were on location. For the first day's shoot, cast and crew convened at Allsop Place, off Baker Street in London's West End. As the location was just a short hop from Paul's St. John's Wood residence, Paul was there early to supervise the boarding of the bus. As would be expected, there was plenty of hanging around, and the Beatle spent some moments with fellow cast member and poet Ivor Cutler on the street and in a nearby transport cafe. After much delay waiting for the bus to arrive (it was being hastily decorated in psychedelic livery), they were ready to leave.

Paul: "We've been waiting for a couple of years now to make another feature film, and we've been asking people to write stories and write plots. But nobody's come up with one, you know. So we thought we'll do something which isn't like a real film. . . . We'd put together a lot of things that we like the look of and see what happens."

IVOR AND HE

Despite the nonappearance of the magical bus, Paul happily shared some tarmac with Ivor Cutler (seated next to
Paul). The offbeat Scottish poet cum
avant-garde raconteur was simpatico
with the nebulous ambitions of *Magical
Mystery Tour,* and his cameo spot as
Buster Bloodvessel, the coach's ersatz
courier, was one of the few highlights
of the film.

September 11, 1967

ONBOARD AND READY TO ROLL
Because of their suburban location, it
was deemed more appropriate for
Ringo, John, and George to be picked
up en route from the nearby Surrey
hamlet of Virginia Water rather than
scuttle into London. One embarrassing
detail that had been left off the preproduction itinerary (among many
other things) was to order a set of
duplicate clothes for the principal cast
members. This omission meant that
the same clothes had to be worn
throughout the five days of filming.

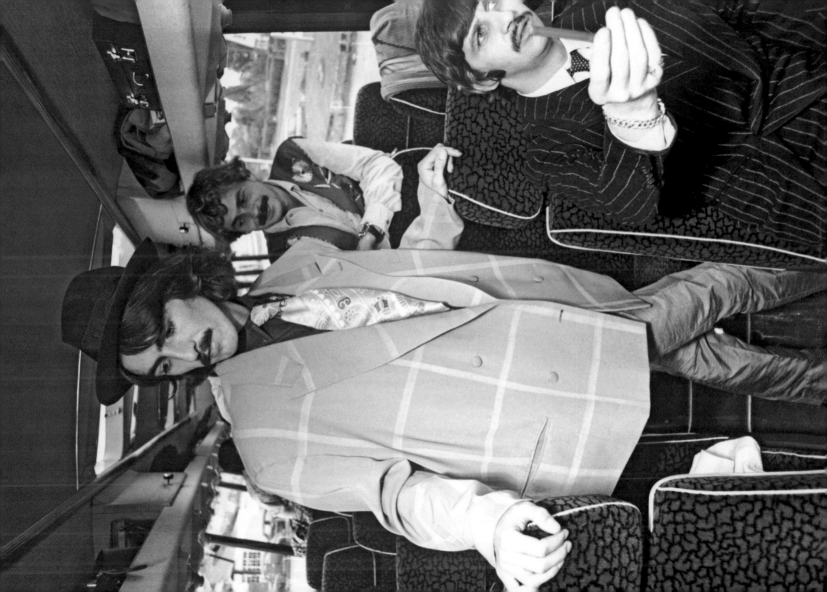

September 11, 1967

HAPPY SNAPPER

Paul takes a few moments off the bus
to play with a Russian Photo-Sniper
camera. Because of heightened sensi-
tivities from their prodigious drug use
and cosmic mind expansion, it was
interpreted that Paul's ambitious ideas
for the film were a takeover bid, especially in the wake of Brian's death.
Paul, however, was keen to stress that
he had the band's best interests at
heart.

Paul: "John said *Magical Mystery Tour*
was 'just a big ego trip for Paul.' God,
it was for their sake, to keep us together,
keep us going, give us something
new to do."

September 11, 1967

MAGICAL MYSTERY BORE

John waiting patiently for the magic
to begin. He and George had been
less than keen to do the film but had
acquiesced during the maelstrom
following Brian's death.

John: "George and I were sort of
grumbling about the fucking movie,
but we thought we'd better do it as we
had the feeling we owed it to the public
to do these daft things."

September 12, 1967

A modest but enthusiastic crowd
greeted the Beatles' arrival in Plymouth
after an eventful morning filming in
the area. Decked out in their film costumes, the group signed a few autographs and spoke briefly to a BBC
news team who were compiling a feature on the group's antics in the region.

Q: "What's it all about then?"

Paul (sings): "It's a mystery to me!"

September 12, 1967

TEA ON THE HOE

The Beatles relax on the greenery
of Plymouth Hoe, a large expanse of
grass in front of the West Country
coastline. The Beatles' morning had
been nothing short of a disaster. They
had planned to film some of the rural
pursuits taking place at the gathering,
but the bus driver had blissfully ignored
the "maximum seven-foot width" sign
on a bridge they had to cross, and the
bus became wedged between the sides
of the bridge, effectively putting an
end to filming that day. With the large
contingent of media and fans in its
wake now in chaos, the bus backed off
the bridge and headed for the relative
peace of Plymouth.

Neil Aspinall: "What we should
have been filming was the chaos we
caused—the bus trying to get over this
narrow bridge, with queues of traffic
building up behind us, and then having
to reverse and go back past all the
drivers who'd been cursing us, and
John getting off in a fury and ripping
all the posters off the sides."

September 13, 1967

ON THE BEACH AT NEWQUAY
The Beatles' two previous films were
made under the supervision of the giant
United Artists corporation. Under UA's
stewardship, months would have gone
into the preparation of a film, with
every little detail, from daily call sheets,
accommodations, costumes, and cater-
ing taken care of. For *Magical Mystery
Tour*, there was little in the way of
organization or preparation with the
hope that some love-generation bonhomie would extend to both cast and
crew. On the morning of September
13, the filming party convened on
Newquay Beach in Cornwall to shoot
some ad hoc sequences and ended up
including some curious vacationers in
the frame.

September 13, 1967

WAITING FOR THE MAGIC

While Paul was up to his magical mystery antics on Newquay Beach, John preferred to take a few paces back and watch the proceedings from a distance. The legacy of Brian Epstein's death, the Beatles temporary abandonment of drugs, and the new influence of transcendental meditation meant that John was uncharacteristically passive during this period of the Beatles' history and acquiesced to Paul's steerage of the group.

September 13, 1967

I AM THE DIRECTOR

After a morning's frolick on the beach
at Newquay, the crew repaired to the
swimming pool at the rear of the
Atlantic Hotel for John's directorial
debut. Employing a cast of glamor
girls, the venerable comic actor Nat
"Rubber Man" Jackley, and an accor-
dian player named Shirley Evans, the
scene (ostensibly a dream sequence) was
filmed with much jocularity despite the
light September chill. For all the effort
expended that day, the sequence would
be unceremoniously junked from the
final cut and to this day has never
been seen.

September 14, 1967

OUT IN THE FIELD
Day five of the *Magical Mystery Tour*
shoot and there is still enough enthusi-
asm left for a romp around a West
Country field. One scene required a
tent set up in a field where the cast
would go to "disappear"; in the next
scene they are in a cinema to the strains
of George's composition, "Blue Jay
Way." A freshly cut wheat field was
found outside Newquay and was
deemed suitable for the purpose of
engaging the cast in a bit of meandering for the camera.

CAMPING IT UP

John, followed by Little Nicola Hale, makes his way out of the tent as the cameraman focuses in. As *Magical Mystery Tour* had little or no script, many of the scenes shot were taken on the spur of the moment with the hope that they would slot into the collage of nondescript film footage the Beatles had collected during their travels. This sequence segued into George's song "Blue Jay Way," a paean to a misty, hallucinogenic night in Los Angeles.

George: "Derek Taylor [Beatles press agent] got held up. He rang to say he'd be late. I told him on the phone that the house was in Blue Jay Way. And he said he could find it okay . . . he could always ask a cop. So I waited and waited. I felt really knackered with the flight, but I didn't want to go to sleep until he came. There was a fog and it got later and later. To keep myself awake, just as a joke to pass the time, I wrote a song about waiting for him in Blue Jay Way. There was a little Hammond organ in the corner of this house which I hadn't noticed until then . . . so I messed around on it and the song came."

September 18, 1967

RED LIGHT
The Beatles relax under the heavy
drapes of Paul Raymond's Revue Bar
in Soho. The gentleman's club was the
setting for a scene intended to add a
steamy dimension to the psychedelic
shenanigans in *Magical Mystery Tour*.
The Beatles and various male members
of the cast found themselves entertained by stripper Jan Carson and the
fantastic Bonzo Dog Doo-Dah Band.

Mid-September 1967

RINGO AT THE WHEEL

By 1967 the Beatles were used to
organizations giving in to their
demands at the drop of a check, but
when they planned to film their giant
finale sequence at Shepperton studios
at the eleventh hour, they were to be
disappointed; the studio had been
booked for weeks. Instead, the group
had the novel idea of taking over a
vast aircraft hanger based at West
Malling in Kent to host several large
interior sequences. While at the airfield complex, the group took full
advantage of the grounds, runway,
and associated aviation structures.
During one bizarre sequence, Ringo
took over the driving of the *Magical
Mystery Tour* bus for a race around the
airfield's lengthy runway.

October 18, 1967

A newly restored vintage Hispano-
Suiza whisks Paul, George, and Pattie
out of London's West End after the
premiere of John's first solo film
appearance in *How I Won the War*.
Although the movie was filmed in late
1966, critics had to wait more than a
year to judge John's first solo venture
outside the Beatles, and although they
were dismissive of the film's preten-
sions, they were mildly upbeat about
John's performance. The event prompted appearances by a large number of
swinging London's illuminati with the
likes of David Hemmings, Cilla Black,
Cass Elliot, and Jimi Hendrix donning
their best to catch the starlight on the
film's opening night.

November 10, 1967

GOODBYE . . . HELLO?

It had only been 48 months since
they'd last worn them, but it might
well have been 46 years. The Beatles
briefly dipped into the past to try on
their old Pierre Cardin collarless tunics
for a promotional slot for their new
single "Hello Goodbye." The film, shot
at the Saville Theatre, ran into several
problems with the Musicians' Union,
as the group was clearly miming to a
recording of the song (a taboo practice
in 1967).

December 5, 1967

THE FOOL ON THE WALL

The Apple shop, the first tangible manifestation of Apple, the company set up by the Beatles to divert some of the inordinate taxes the group was handing over to the government each year. On sound advice, the boys had taken over the lease of a shop at 94 Baker Street in London and had planned to fill it with groovy merchandise for themselves, their friends, and, by extension, the hordes of fans who'd want to shop at the most exclusive address in London. A team of psychedelic minstrels cum artists known as the Fool was employed to decorate the interior and exterior of the shop. If nothing else, the finished result was in keeping with the experimental mood of the times. The opening night in early December saw John and George attending the festivities. The press labeled it a "Psychedelic 'Garden of Eden,'" while Baker Street's proprietors were scratching their heads in dismay.

Ringo could be excused for missing the opening of the Apple shop as he was away in Rome filming his first substantial movie role outside the Beatles. For his part in the "sexploitation" film *Candy*, Ringo turned in a believable cameo as a sex-mad gardener leching after the beautiful Candy (played by Swedish beauty queen Ewa Aulin). The 12-day jaunt gave Ringo plenty of time to relax in the company of such movie-land jet-setters as Richard Burton, Marlon Brando, and boxer Sugar Ray Leonard.

Ringo: "I took *Candy* because it wasn't too big a part and there was (sic) other stars: Marlon Brando, Richard Burton, and Peter Sellers. I thought, 'They will be carrying the film, not me, and I'll learn from them.'"

December 27, 1967

THE DAY AFTER THE NIGHT BEFORE
Paul, flanked by his loyal father, Jim, meets the press to defend *Magical Mystery Tour*. The film had premiered on BBC 1 at peak time during the Boxing Day celebrations and was met with a torrent of poor notices from the critics. Despite the apparent "home movie" feel of the picture, the film would have benefited from a screening in color; something to which British television had yet to fully convert. Moreover, the backlash from the press owed more to the controversy the group had stockpiled throughout the year, and for that, the press was more than happy to bash the film on every level.

Paul: "Was the film really all that bad, compared to the rest of Christmas TV? You could hardly call the Queen's speech a gasser. We could put on a mop-top show, but we really don't like that sort of entertainment anymore. We could have sung carols and done a first-class Christmas-y show starring 'The Beatles' with lots of phony tinsel like everyone else. It would have been the easiest thing in the world, but we wanted to do something different. So maybe we boobed; maybe we didn't. We don't say it was a good film. It was our first attempt. If we goofed, then we goofed. It was a challenge and it didn't come off. We'll know better next time."

Colliding Circles, 1968–1970 and Beyond

"There's a beautiful story Yoko told me about a Japanese monk. . . . He loved this fantastic golden temple so much that he didn't want to see it disintegrate. So he burned it. That is what I did with the Beatles. I never wanted them to slide down, making comebacks."

—*John Lennon*

"The Beatle way of life was like a young kid entering the big world, entering it with friends and conquering it totally. And that was fantastic. An incredible experience. So when that idea really came that we should break up, I don't think any of us wanted to accept it. It was the end of the legend, even in our own minds."

—*Paul McCartney*

"I get on well with Ringo and John, and I try my best to get on well with Paul. . . . It's just a matter of time, you know, just for everybody to work out their own problems, and once they've done that I'm sure we'll get back around the cycle again. But if not, you know, it's still all right. Whatever happens, you know, it's going to be okay."

—*George Harrison*

"Someone pointed out that since we broke up, the only way we can all go is downhill because individually none of us will attain what we attained together. And I think that's a very nice statement. And it wasn't derogatory or anything, but it's a fact of life, you know."

—*Ringo Starr*

January 10, 1968

EASTERN VIBES, BOMBAY BEATLE

More at home with a coterie of fine
Indian musicians than with his fellow
Scousers, George made his third trip to
India in the space of just 15 months to
record music for the film *Wonderwall*.
George was commissioned to do the
music by director Joe Massot and
characteristically leapt at the chance to
fully immerse himself in the musical
vibrations that only India could offer.
While in Bombay, he would also lay
down the backing track to his sublime
work "The Inner Light," which would
end up as the B-side to the Beatles'
next single, "Lady Madonna."

George: "I'm a musician and I don't
know why. Many people feel that life is
predestined. I think it is vaguely, but
it's still up to the person which way
your life is going to go. All I've ever
done is keep being me, and it's all
worked out . . . like magic. I never
planned anything, so it's obvious that
that's what I am destined to be. I'm a
musician. It's my gig."

January 16, 1968

With a Russian fur hat protecting him
from the chill, George alights from
his Air-India plane at Heathrow. With
the Beatles' complex business details
becoming more and more tangled
since Epstein's death, George's gentle
demeanor would be sorely tested in the
coming months. India's charms would
soon be calling George back, and
within the month, he would be returning to his beloved, newly adopted
spiritual home.

February 15, 1968

From left: John, his wife Cynthia,
George, Jenny Boyd (Pattie's sister),
and George's wife Pattie, waiting for
clearance to board their plane bound
for India and the maharishi's spiritual
hideaway. After their first meeting, the
guru had extended an invitation to the
group to join him in his meditation
sanctuary in the Himalayan village of
Rishikesh. But the death of Brian
Epstein put this much-needed vacation
back a few months. As soon as its commitments were clear, the group wasted
no time in joining the mystic for an
intense three-month retreat.

April 18, 1968

Backstage at the Adelphi Theatre in
London's West End, John and Ringo
support fellow Merseybeat traveler
Gerry Marsden after his debut in the
variety show *Charlie Girl*. The celebrated
Pacemaker—seen here with actor and
Hard Day's Night veteran, Derek
Nimmo—never had the staying power
to last beyond Merseymania and
found his niche more in cabaret than
psychedelia.

May 11, 1968

A IS FOR APPLE

Paul and John tease the press at
London's Heathrow with their new
company logo. John and Paul were en
route to New York to formally launch
Apple, the Beatles' attempt at what
Paul defined as their slant on "Western
Communism." John and Paul were
united in their vision of a Beatles'
utopia, in which new talent would be
given a chance at wealth and fame
without the constraints of big business.

John: "It's a company we're setting up
involving records, films, and electron-
ics, and as a sideline, manufacturing or
whatever. We want to set up a system
where people who just want to make a
film about anything don't have to go
on their knees in somebody's office.
Probably yours."

Paul: "It's just trying to mix business
with enjoyment. We're in the happy
position of not needing any more
money. So for the first time, the bosses
aren't in it for profit. We've already
bought all our dreams. We want to
share that possibility with others."

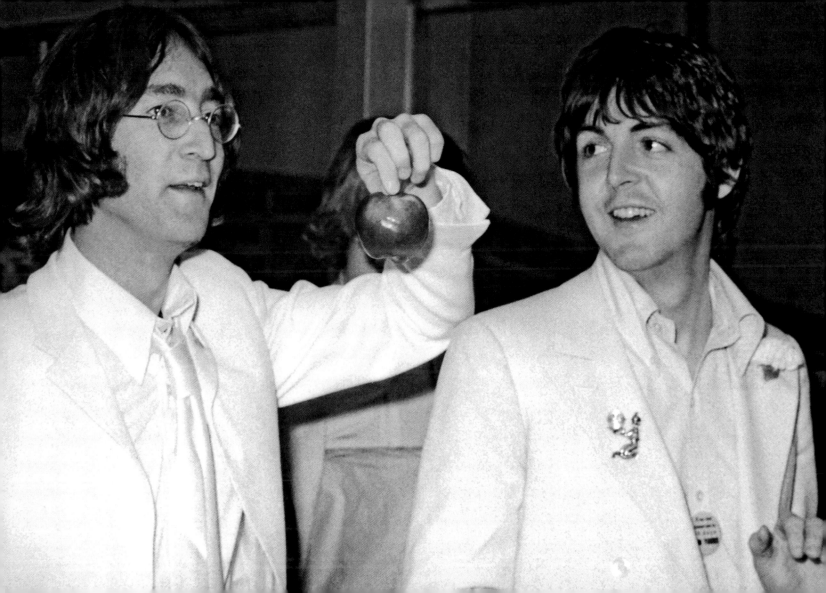

May 18, 1968 (this page)   May 16, 1968 (opposite)

While John and Paul were in the
States, George and Ringo were taking in the Mediterranean glitz of the
Cannes Film Festival. Ringo and
wife Maureen (this page) leaving the
restaurant Moucho, a popular hang-
out for Cannes festivalgoers in the
old quarter of the French Riviera
town. Ringo in particular enjoyed
the atmosphere surrounding the
Cannes festival, as it made for a
welcome diversion from the interminable business dealings and
squabbles that were engulfing the
Beatles at home. Since both Ringo's
cameo role in the film *Candy* and
George's soundtrack debut on
Wonderwall were being premiered
at the festival, it was to be more
of a working holiday than a break.
George and wife Pattie (opposite) at
London Airport on their way to the
Cannes Film Festival.

May 18, 1968

MEETING MR. POLANSKI

Ringo spent a few hassle-free days at
the Cannes Film Festival helping to
promote the film *Candy*. During the
evening of May 18, Ringo and wife
Maureen had been to see the British
film *Joanna*, directed by Mike Sarne.
After the screening the couple hitched
up with Polish director Roman
Polanski for a chat. Polanski and the
Beatles' paths would cross several
times over the years, although the
relationship was publicly sullied by the
inference that the group's "White
Album" was somehow influential in
the bloody death of the director's
wife, Sharon Tate, at the hands of
Charles Manson and his "family."

May 22, 1968

John and George in a huddle after the
opening of another Apple shop. The
Beatles, privy to the esoteric require-
ments of the drama community, had
opened a second shop named Apple
Tailoring (Civil and Theatrical) at
161 King's Road in Chelsea, London.
The shop seemed much more thoroughly researched than its chaotic
sister shop on Baker Street, and was
quite successful in providing sartorial
accessories to the theatrical profession.
The two Beatles attended the opening
of the King's Road store, then walked
up the street to the swanky Club Dell
Aretusa, where they enjoyed a post-
launch reception. John took this
opportunity to invite his new partner,
Japanese avant-garde artist Yoko Ono,
to the gathering, causing ripples of
speculation as to the whereabouts
of his wife Cynthia. This was John and
Yoko's first outing together in public.

John: "I'm not talking about my
marriage. I don't want to say anything
about it. It complicates matters."

July 1, 1968

YOU ARE HERE

John and Yoko at the *You Are Here* exhibition at Robert Fraser's West End gallery. As this was John's first solo art venture, he took the opportunity to be photographed with his new partner, Yoko Ono. As a noted conceptual artist herself, Yoko was simpatico with the creative side of the errant Beatle's brain and encouraged him to assert his talent independently of the other Beatles. John would celebrate this first artistic venture with the release of 365 balloons into the London sky. John was gung-ho about the event, even if it meant alienating his ever growing legion of critics.

John: "Putting it on was taking a swipe at [the critics] in a way. I mean, that's what it was about. What they couldn't understand was that a lot of them were saying, 'Well, if it hadn't been for John Lennon nobody would have gone to it,' but as it was, it was me doing it. And if it had been 'Sam Bloggs' it would have been nice. But the point of it was—it was me. And they're using that as a reason to say why it didn't work. Work as what?"

EVERY ONE OF US

Work had finally been completed on
the postproduction of *Yellow Submarine,*
and, for the benefit of the press, a
launch was held at a small viewing
theater at Bowater House in Knightsbridge, London. George, Paul, and
Ringo parried the journalists' questions
about the film, their first celluloid
endeavor since the troubled *Magical
Mystery Tour.* John, mindful of the
speculation about his relationship with
Yoko Ono, skipped the event.

Paul: "We're just in it as drawings.
It's us animated."

Q: "Did *Magical Mystery Tour* put
you off making a film completely
yourselves?"

George: "Yeah, we're going to be
cartoons forever now, because they
really put us off. Those no-good,
damn critics."

YELLOW SUBMARINE LAUNCH

Yellow Submarine was a welcome reaf-
firmation of the cozy Beatles' image
much loved by press and public. The
whimsical nature of the film opened
up yet another market as preteens
flocked to the movies to wallow in the
childlike imagery. In reality, the Beatles
had little to do with the finished product; four mimics, including the British
television comedian Dick Emery, provided their voices, while the Beatles'
musical contribution to the soundtrack
consisted of a hodgepodge of outtakes
and previously released material. But
the press and public loved it, and for a
short while at least, the Beatles were
back in favor.

Roger Ebert (film critic): "[It]
is the most original and inventive
feature-length animated cartoon since
the days when Walt Disney was still
thinking up innovations."

July 17, 1968

"WHERE'S YOUR WIFE?"
The anticipation leading up to the
release of *Yellow Submarine* was palpable, and the chaos that prevailed in
London's Piccadilly Circus on the day
of the premiere was a throwback to
the halcyon days of Beatlemania. The
four Beatles arrived at the London
Pavilion Cinema to a tumultuous welcome. However, garnering the majority
of column space the next morning was
John, who arrived entwined with Yoko
Ono. The press was on his case, shouting out to John about his wife's absence.

Reporter: "Where's your wife?"

John: "I don't know."

DEJA VU ALL OVER AGAIN

Piccadilly Circus hadn't seen anything like this since, well, the last Beatles film premiere back in 1965 for *Help!* The fans ensured that there was plenty of that Beatlemania spirit to be had for the *Yellow Submarine* opening. Paul, ever the publicist, munched on an apple for the benefit of the cameras, although it was noted that in addition to the controversy surrounding John's marital shift, Paul had arrived alone, without his long-standing girlfriend, Jane Asher. A few days later Asher announced that their five-year relationship was over.

Jane Asher: "It's finished. . . . I don't really want to talk about it."

July 17, 1968

GEORGE AND PATTIE

George and wife Pattie looked every
bit the swinging couple as they arrived
for the *Yellow Submarine* launch. Signi-
ficantly, this was George's last public
event with the rest of the group; his
Beatle image was becoming more
and more at odds with his newly
discovered self.

George: "When it's in the midst of
all this and people are saying 'Beatles
this' and 'Beatles that,' then I've got to
accept the thing that they think I'm a
Beatle. I'm willing to go along with it,
you know, if they want me to be a
Beatle, then I'll be one."

July 26, 1968

APPLE IN ACTION

The initial Apple decree to ferret out new talent found its first success with Mary Hopkin. The diminutive 18-year-old singer had appeared on the popular TV talent show, *Opportunity Knocks*. It was there that she was spotted by the fashion model, Twiggy. She promptly rang Paul, who, impressed by the Welsh woman's rich Celtic tones, had the teenager record a reworked version of the Russian folk song, "Those Were the Days." With the Beatles' patronage, it scaled the heights of the pop charts to number one.

John: "If somebody wants to make a film, they normally get shown into the wastepaper bin, and nothing ever happens, and people never see it. We hope to make a thing that's free, where people can just come, and do, and record . . . and not have to ask, 'Can we have another mic in the studio?' just because they haven't had a hit."

"JUST ONE ITEM PER PERSON"

For more than six months, the shop owners of Baker Street were incandescent in their condemnation of the gigantic psychedelic mural that had been painted on the side of the Beatles' trendy Apple shop. Under an avalanche of complaints, the powers that be pressured the shop's management to have it removed, replacing it with a stark whitewash. The boutique's initial success was not reflected in the cash registers however, and amid accusations of pilfering, the plug was pulled on the shop. In keeping with the spirit of the times, it was decided that the remainder of the stock be given away to the general public.

The "great giveaway" provoked chaotic scenes in and around Baker Street and the police were called in to restore order. A couple of days later, Paul and a few friends went to the vacant premises late at night and, after slapping white paint over the windows, traced the titles of the Beatles' new singles, "Hey Jude" and "Revolution," into the glass. In his excitement, Paul had overlooked the large Jewish community in the area who took considerable exception at the (wholly innocent) anti-Semitic inference.

Paul: "We decided to close down the shop last Saturday, not because it wasn't making any money, but because we thought the retail business wasn't our particular scene. So we went along, chose all the stuff we wanted—I got a smashing overcoat—and then told our friends. Now everything that is left is for the public."

THE CARNIVAL IS OVER

John with Yoko at Marylebone Court to face charges for the possession of marijuana and obstructing the police. Although the Beatles had publicly foresworn narcotics during their fling with the maharishi, it was no secret within certain circles that their appetite for marijuana was as healthy as ever. Privy to these mutterings was Detective Sergeant Pilcher, whose stock-in-trade was to raid high-profile rock stars in possession of their personal preferences. Without the mighty Epstein to pull the establishment's strings, the Beatles were now vulnerable to the forces of the law, and John was arrested for possessing cannabis during a raid on the couple's flat in London's Montague Square.

Derek Taylor (Apple press officer): "The evening papers arrived. 'Lennon and Yoko' was the main story. Not John anymore, 'Lennon.' A fan called, tearfully, for news and said, 'God bless you.' Mick Jagger was phoned and told on the set of his movie. He offered advice and love. Brian Jones called and sympathized. Now we're truly all one and the Beatles were as persona non Scotland Yard grata as the Stones."

John: "As this stuff is all mine, it will be me only who is involved."

November 8, 1968

A somber and diminutive Cynthia
Lennon arrives at the High Court
with her solicitor for the divorce hearing against husband John. It was a
difficult time all around for John's
former partner, although in the face
of all the public frolicking of John
and Yoko it was no real surprise that
Cynthia was awarded a *decree nisi*
in her case.

Cynthia Lennon: "I couldn't
believe that it was happening to me. I
hadn't even had a chance to discuss
anything with John. I was being cut
off like a gangrenous limb with the
speed of a surgeon's scalpel."

November 21, 1968

YOKO MISCARRIES

During October, John had announced
to the press that Yoko was pregnant
with their first child, although it was
obvious to those close to the couple
that the circumstances surrounding the
pregnancy weren't at all conducive to a
safe delivery. Certainly, the harrowing
drug raid in October and venomous
press campaign against the pair had a
considerable emotional effect on Yoko:
Yoko had nearly lost the baby after the
drug raid. Four weeks later Yoko was
again rushed to the hospital, and
despite the efforts of specialists at
Queen Charlotte's Maternity Hospital,
it was apparent that the child would
not carry to full term. John stayed with
Yoko for the duration of her time in
the hospital, sleeping in a neighboring
bed. When it was discovered that the
bed was needed urgently by an incom-
ing patient, John slept on a collection
of pillows on the floor alongside Yoko's
bed. The miscarried child was buried
in a location known only to the couple,
and was posthumously named John
Ono Lennon.

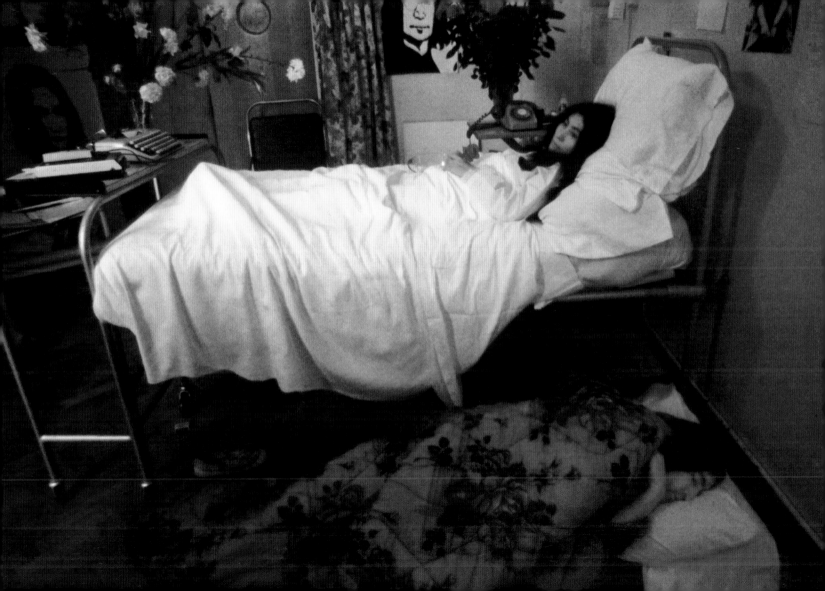

REAL LOVE

Despite the high-profile activities of John and Yoko, no one could deny that their love was genuine. This is one of a series of photos taken at John's home, Kenwood, as it was being cleared prior to its sale. The photos convey a portrait of a couple very much in love.

John: "We both think alike. We've both been alone. And we seem to have had the same kind of dreams when we were alone. I can see now that I always dreamed of a woman like this coming into my life. You can't go out looking for this kind of relationship. It's like somebody was planning it from above."

December 1968

BATHISM
John and Yoko keep it clean in the bathtub. Such was the nature of John and Yoko's union that they decreed to keep a visual as well as an audio diary of their time together (a tradition that was maintained right up to John's death in 1980). The photographer, Susan Wood, followed the couple during their early months together and recorded the highs and lows of this remarkable convergence of kindred spirits.

John: "I don't regret a thing, you know? Especially since meeting Yoko. That's made everything worthwhile."

Q: "What especially attracted you to Yoko?"

John: "Well, she's me in drag."

December 11, 1968

John and Yoko ham it up for the Rolling
Stones' TV special *Rock and Roll Circus*.
The show featured a star-studded
gallery of 1960s rock icons, including
Jethro Tull, Marianne Faithfull, and the
Who. Certainly feeling like an outsider,
John gleefully accepted an offer to
appear on the show without the other
Beatles and played in a jam session with
Keith Richards, Eric Clapton, and Jimi
Hendrix's drummer, Mitch Mitchell
(the scratch quintet billed as A.N.Other).
With additional accompaniment from
what John described as "a mad violin
player" and yelps and squeals from
Yoko, the group played a storming
version of the Beatles' "White Album"
track "Yer Blues."

December 11, 1968

DAD FOR THE DAY

John and Yoko hung around the set for the majority of the *Rock and Roll Circus* performances and appeared in a few audience scenes, raving along to the likes of Jethro Tull and the Who. It wasn't all rock 'n' roll shenanigans though; there were a few poignant moments, as when John's estranged son, Julian, visited the studios to be with his dad for the day.

WALKING OUT

A resolute George leaves Twickenham studios with long-serving Beatles aide Mal Evans at the wheel. For most of January 1969, George had been rehearsing with the other Beatles for a projected live show—the group's first in more than three years—while their preparations were being filmed for a television special. Although initially acquiescent to the idea, the sensitive Beatle quickly found the tension on set upsetting to his delicate antennas. George had been in a relatively good space since returning from time abroad in the States with Bob Dylan, yet the atmosphere at Twickenham was a complete contrast to the gentle bonhomie he found with Dylan. George had to endure John and Yoko's ever-encroaching liaison, but it was Paul who finally caused George to snap, and a full-blown argument played itself out in the studio.

George: "In normal circumstances, I had not let his attitude bother me and, to get a peaceful life, I had always let him have his own way, even when it meant that songs that I had composed were not being recorded. When I came back from the U.S. . . . I was in a very happy frame of mind, but I quickly discovered that I was up against the same old Paul. In front of the camera, as we were actually being filmed, Paul started to get at me about the way I was playing."

ONE LAST TIME

Despite the internal fracas, George was eventually coaxed back to finish the Beatles' film project, which was directed by Michael Lindsay Hogg. Any hopes of a live concert as such were ditched, however. Gone, too, was Twickenham studios—its cold, uninviting sound stages making rock 'n' roll at ten in the morning a thoroughly unrewarding exercise. All four Beatles agreed that their newly completed studio under the Apple headquarters on Savile Row was a cozier option. In their absence, "Magic" Alex, Apple's in-house electrician, had designed a state-of-the-art recording complex and the Beatles were keen to explore the Greek inventor's far-out innovations.

However, in reality, very little of the Greek's blueprints made it off the drawing board, and as a result, precious little material was completed during the sessions. Even then, most of what survived was captured on an EMI mobile console, drafted in to compensate for the inadequacies of the machinery. An eleventh-hour proposal to film an impromptu performance on the roof of the Apple building was surprisingly agreed upon by the Beatles. On the morning of January 30, the group played a spirited set of ten songs from their current sessions, despite the January chill. Ultimately, though, despite the occasion of the Beatles' last ever "live" performance, the noise pollution from 42 minutes of amplified Beatles music caused considerable consternation in the district, and the police were called to restore the peace.

John: "I'd like to say 'thank you' on behalf of the group and ourselves and I hope we've passed the audition."

March 11, 1969

SOMETHING IS HAPPENING

Paul arriving at Apple's headquarters
the day before his marriage to Linda
Eastman. Word had leaked out (by
none other than Paul himself) that the
last Beatle was to tie the knot. Paul was
typically coy about the fact that the
news had escaped and happily played a
game of cat-and-mouse with the press
as they pursued him for what ended up
being the last comments they would
receive from a single Beatle. His bride-
to-be, Linda, had been busy too,
popping into Marylebone Registry
Office to give the requisite 24-hour
notice of their impending union.

Paul: "Yes, it's true, I am getting
married. But I'm saying nothing
more at the minute."

March 11, 1969

THOSE WEDDING BELLS

After an evening producing Apple's
latest discovery, Jackie Lomax, Paul
braved the waiting press, fans, and
well-wishers as he made his way back
to his St. John's Wood home. One pre-
marital duty he'd neglected to attend to
was the purchase of the wedding rings;
in the small hours, Paul knocked on the
door of a jeweler to purchase them,
costing him the princely sum of £12
in the process.

March 11, 1969

Paul lays the law down to fans and
press as he leaves Apple headquarters to
make the short trip home to his home
in St. John's Wood. Paul was characteristically enjoying the fuss that was
surrounding his marriage.

March 11, 1969

Before turning in for the night, Paul still had to deal with the press and fans who had gathered outside his Cavendish Avenue house. Paul's impending nuptials were too much for a group of fans, later to become immortalized in song as the "Apple Scruffs." During the latter part of the 1960s, the band of obsessed fans spent their waking hours waiting for the Beatles to appear from their various offices and studios in the hope of receiving a brief word or a nod from their idols. To the section of the pack known as "Paul's girls," the news that their favorite and long unattached Beatle was to marry was a devastating blow.

Carol Bedford (Apple Scruff): "I could tell just from their faces that the girls would never accept Linda. Nor would they ever accept Paul getting married. He was theirs and they were his girls. As long as he was single, there was hope you might be the one. . . . They each felt they were a special part of his life and this was about to end."

March 12, 1969

IT'S OVER!
Paul and Linda McCartney descend the
steps of Marylebone Registry Office to
a phenomenal welcome from press and
fans. The wedding, initially booked for
9:45 a.m., was delayed for an hour by
the late appearance of Paul's brother,
Mike, who had been held up by a late
train from Liverpool. In the event, no
other marriages were scheduled that
day and so the McCartneys' appointment was honored without too much
fuss. Despite having leaked the news
to the press, Paul was still a little
nonplussed at the attention the wedding was receiving.

Paul: "All I wanted was a quiet ceremony between Linda and myself. It
doesn't concern anybody else."

March 12, 1969

In the car after the wedding, Paul and Linda, with Linda's daughter, Heather, and Paul's brother, Michael, ease their way through the crowd en route to a church blessing. With them, to their left, is Apple boss and witness Peter Brown. Seconds after this picture was taken, the side window of the car was shattered under the weight of people trying to get a closer look at the couple.

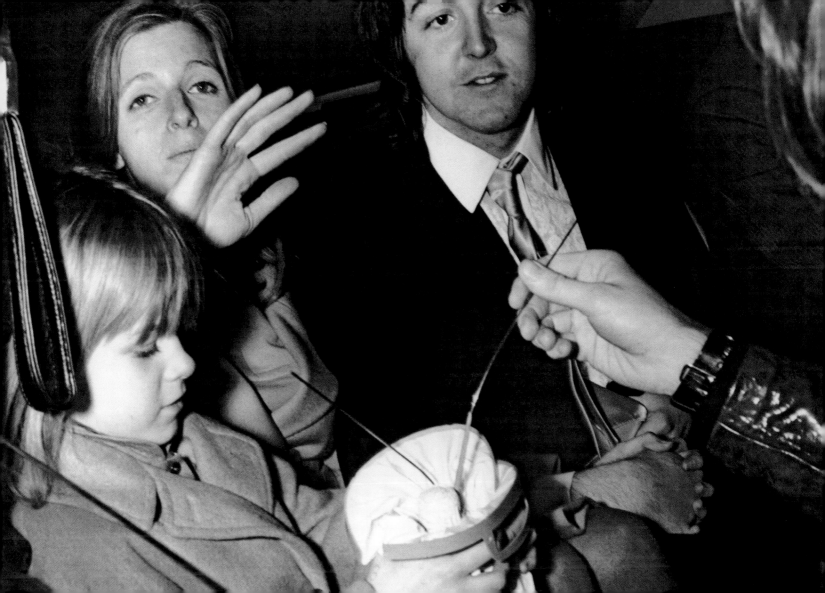

Linda relaxes on Paul's shoulder after
their hectic schedule. The couple were
front-page news that evening after their
high-profile union. Despite the celebrations, many of Paul's fans were enraged
that he married Linda.

March 12, 1969

After the wedding ceremony, Paul and Linda made a trip to a St. John's Wood church for a traditional blessing. Shortly afterward, with Linda's daughter, Heather, in tow, the happy family repaired to the swank Ritz Hotel, in London's Piccadilly Circus, to give a few interviews to the various news agencies.

Q: "Paul, what does it feel like to be married at last?"

Paul: "It feels fine, thank you."

Q: "Is this going to change your life much, do you think?"

Paul: "I don't know, really. I've never been married before."

Q: "When did you decide to get married, and what prompted it?"

Paul: "About a week ago. We just decided to do it rather than think about it."

Q: "How do you feel about being father to a six-year-old?"

Paul (jokingly): "It's terrible. I hate it!"

It was then back to Paul's house in St. John's Wood, where a few jubilant fans showered the couple with confetti as they entered the green doors to the property.

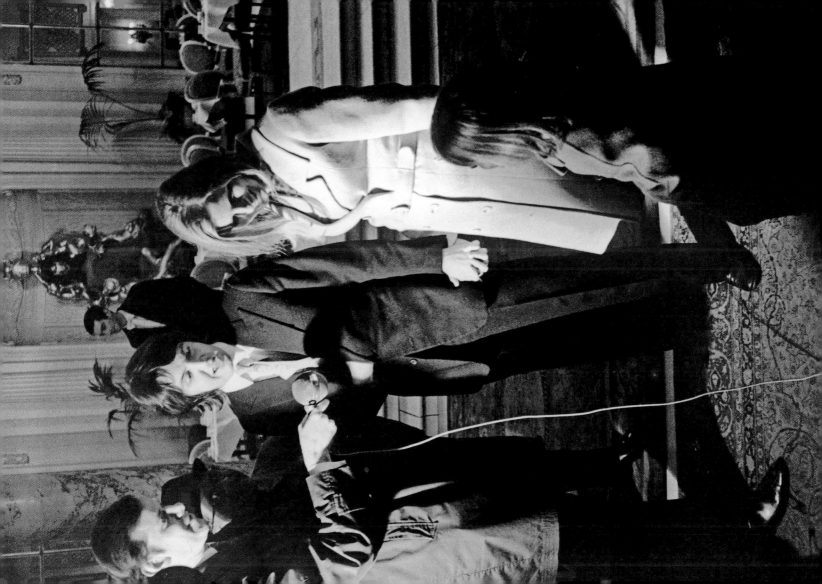

ONE LAST WORD

Once they arrived home at Paul's St.
John's Wood property, there was still
more press to attend to and the newlyweds gave a final interview on their
doorstep. With Paul's dog, Martha,
barking in the background and a
phalanx of militant fans hollering
over the 12-foot wall, it proved to be
a somewhat chaotic, noisy exchange.

Q: "Mrs. McCartney, congratulations!
What does it feel like to get married to
one of the most eligible bachelors in the
world and be the envy of all the ladies?"

Linda: "Well, it feels great to be
married."

March 20, 1969

IT'S LEGAL

As if proof was needed, John and Yoko's love for each other was now legally binding. On the tarmac of the Gibraltar Airport, John proudly displays the wedding certificate, newly obtained from the offices of the British consulate. The couple had flown to Gibraltar from Paris upon learning that they could marry there in relative secrecy. Their love affair with the pretty British quarter was short-lived, though, and they spent just 70 minutes in the territory with Apple aide Peter Brown and Apple photographer David Nuttall as witnesses.

City and Garrison
of GIBRALTAR.

A 15697

Fee : 2s. 6d.

Search Fee : Nil.

CERTIFIED COPY of an ENTRY OF MARRIAGE
Pursuant to the Marriage Ordinance

in the City of Gibraltar.

1969   Marriage   contracted at the Registrar's Office

No.	When Married.	Name and Surname.	Age.	Condition.	Rank or Profession	Residence at the time of Marriage.	Father's Name and Surname.	Rank or Profession of Father.	Insert in this Margin any Notes which appear in the original entry.
308	Twentieth March, 1969.	JOHN WINSTON LENNON	28	Previous marriage dissolved	Musician Composer	Kenwood, Cavendish Drive, Waybridge, Surrey	Alfred Lennon	Seaman (retired)	
		YOKO ONO COX	36	Previous marriage dissolved	Artist	25, Hanover Gate Mansion, London W.1.	Eisuke Ono	Banker (retired)	

Married in the   Registrar's Office, by Governor's Special Licence, before me:

C. J. Wheeler
Marriage Registrar

This Marriage was contracted between us,	John Winston Lennon	in the presence of us.	Peter Brown	- - - - - - -
	Yoko Ono Cox		D. Nutter	

I, CECIL JOSEPH WHEELER - - - - Marriage Registrar of Gibraltar, do hereby certify that this is a true copy of the Entry No. 308 in Volume XVI

of the Register Book of this City and Garrison. Witness my hand and Seal this 20th day of March, 1969

Cecil Joseph Wheeler
Marriage Registrar.

March 20, 1969

FLYING HIGH

John and Yoko prepare to leave Gibraltar
with a photo call against the dramatic
1,398-foot-high Rock of Gibraltar.
With pilot Trevor Copleston at the
controls of their private jet, the newlyweds continued their holiday in Paris.

March 24, 1969

WALKING THE STREETS OF PARIS
John and Yoko wandering around the
artists' quarter of Paris's Left Bank.
The newlyweds, their monochromatic
fashion sense veering between all black
and all white, would meet up with the
surrealist artist, Salvador Dalí, during
their stay. In France at least, they were
allowed a little respite from all the controversy they were facing in England.

John: "I know it won't be very comfortable walking around with all the
lorry drivers whistling and that, but
it'll all die. Next year it'll be nothing,
like miniskirts or bare tits. It isn't anything. We're all naked, really. When
people attack Yoko and me, we know
they're paranoiac. We don't worry too
much. It's the ones that don't know and
you know they don't know, they're just
going round in blue fuzz. The thing
is . . . 'Look, lay off will you? It's two
people, what have we done?'"

March 25, 1969

NUPTIAL PEACE

In the first demonstrable act of their union, John and Yoko staged a "bed-in" for world peace. The couple had flown to Amsterdam to spend seven days in bed in an effort to promote understanding and compassion in the troubled times of 1969. Grabbing the wrong end of the proverbial stick, the world's press converged en masse on the presidential suite of the Amsterdam Hilton, believing that the newlyweds were going to engage in a spot of post-nuptial hanky-panky for the cameras.

John: "Can you think of a better way to spend seven days? It's the best idea we've had."

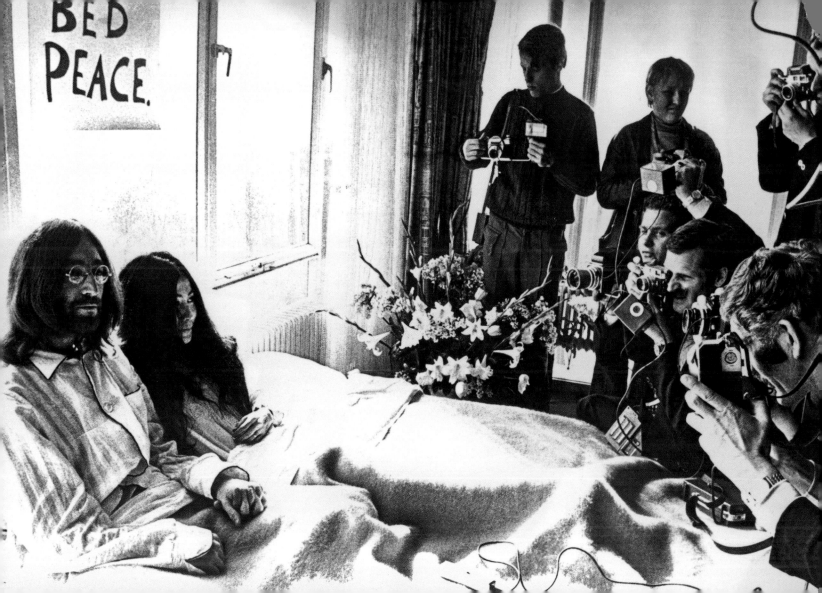

April 1, 1969

THE HONEYMOON IS OVER

John and Yoko arrive back at London's Heathrow after their eventful "honeymoon" in Amsterdam. For all the smiles, John had successfully managed to both enrage and baffle the nation with his antics with Yoko. The metamorphosis from mop-top to psychedelic warrior was not lost on the British press, who pillared his every move with unbridled contempt. His peers back at Apple (although they would never have vocalized it at the time) were similarly confused.

John: "There were some strange reactions from all my friends at Apple about Yoko and me, and what we were doing: 'Have they gone mad?' But of course it was just us, you know, and if they are puzzled or reacting strangely to us two being together and doing what we're doing, it's not hard to visualize the rest of the world really having some amazing image."

April 1, 1969

BED PEACE

Returning from their seven days in
bed for peace, John and Yoko found
time to share some bed-and-bag space
with TV host Eamonn Andrews on
his live early-evening *Today* show.

John: "When Yoko and I were in
Amsterdam doing the bed-in for
peace, we realized that if we have
something to say, or if anybody has
something to say, they can communi-
cate better if they don't confuse anybody with what color their skin is
or how long their hair has grown."

May 4, 1969

When John's last possessions from
Weybridge were finally boxed up,
the whole kit and caboodle was trans-
ported some 20 miles west to Ascot, a
small village famed for its royal horse-
racing connections. John had purchased
Tittenhurst Park, a rambling estate
fronted by an imposing white manor,
for £145,00 in May 1969. The Lennons
soon transformed the house and
grounds into their own personal garden of earthly delights. Among the
new additions was a large lake and a
variety of romantic structures dotted
around the limits of the property. John's
newly found haven would host the
final Beatles' photo session on August
22, 1969.

May 4, 1969

YOU NEVER GIVE ME YOUR MONEY
Ringo and Peter Sellers throw a party
at the exclusive Les Ambassadeurs Club
in London's Mayfair to launch their
new film project, *The Magic Christian*.
The club was familiar territory for
Ringo, as it had hosted several scenes in
A Hard Day's Night. Of all the Beatles,
it was Ringo who felt most at ease
with the jet-set fraternity, and this
evening's guest list included a veritable
who's who of the celebrity set. The
patrons who turned out included fellow Beatles Paul and John, accompanied by Linda and Yoko, and celluloid
luminaries such as Richard Harris,
Roger Moore, Sean Connery, Stanley
Baker, George Peppard, Spike Milligan,
and Christopher Lee.

May 24, 1969

MORE BEDISM

As if seven days in bed for peace in London wasn't enough, John, Yoko, and her daughter, Kyoko, set off from Heathrow for yet another campaign under the linen. Their initial plan to stage the event in America was thwarted due to John's narcotics conviction last October, so the Bahamas (given its close proximity to the U.S.) was chosen. On arrival, however, the unbearable heat made the prospect of seven days in bed an unpleasant thought and unworkable. Undeterred, the couple headed for Montreal, Canada, to begin their peaceful bombardment of America's airwaves and television screens.

SUN, HERE IT COMES

George and wife Pattie fly off to
Sardinia, Spain, for a well-earned holiday. The protracted business dealings of
the Beatles were starting to overshadow
any musical (and spiritual) pursuits
upon which the group was keen to
embark. George in particular was tir-
ing of the interminable squabbling over
the financial mismanagement of the
group and would seek solace in sunnier
climes. It was during this holiday that
he would put the final touches on one
of his most evocative compositions,
"Here Comes the Sun."

George: "We'd been through really
hell with business, and, you know, it
was very heavy. And on that day I just
felt as though I was sagging off, like
from school, it was like that. I just
didn't come in one day. And just the
release of being in the sun—it was
just [a] really nice day. And that song
just came."

June 1, 1969

GIVE PEACE A CHANCE

The culmination of John and Yoko's
high-profile peace crusade from room
1742 of the Queen Elizabeth Hotel in
Montreal was a recording of John's
anthemic composition "Give Peace a
Chance." The simple but effective tune
was recorded in the Lennons' bedroom
with a cast of friends, well-wishers,
and Hare Krishna devotees. Celebrities
Timothy Leary, Tommy Smothers, and
Petula Clark also attended the party,
and happily joined in on the cheering
and clapping toward the end.

John: "I was pleased that America
took up 'Give Peace a Chance' because
I had written it with that in mind,
really. I hoped that instead of singing
'We Shall Overcome' from 1800 or
something, they would have something
contemporary."

GIVE PLEA A CHANCE

As a result of John and Yoko's flag-waving, a sizable contingent of campaigners lobbied for the couple's patronage in their own struggles. One controversy that the couple adopted was the plight of the late James Hanratty, the last man in England to be hung. The circumstances that led to his committal had long been in doubt. John and Yoko had met with Hanratty's family and soon began a short campaign to highlight the suspicions that had been raised over the case.

John: "With the Hanrattys we spent many hours with the parents, and the lawyers, and witnesses that they produced to convince us that there was a miscarriage of justice or a shadow of doubt."

December 10, 1969

DELANEY AND BONNIE AND GEORGE

George arriving in Copenhagen with long-term Beatle aide Mal Evans (at right) for a series of concerts backing Delaney and Bonnie. After a year of stress and torment, George eagerly accepted the offer to go on the road with the American duo for a series of European dates. It was another sign that the Beatles were becoming more and more independent of each other and reaching out beyond the boundaries of the group.

George: "There are no expectations, because it's so anonymous. You can go out and do whatever you can do. I'd like to do this with the Beatles, too, but more like Delaney and Bonnie, with us augmented with a few more singers, and a few trumpets, saxes, organ, and all that."

December 10, 1969

HAPPY IN THE SHADOWS

George onstage with Delaney and
Bonnie at the Falkoner Theatre in
Copenhagan. For the band's series of
gigs throughout Europe, George happily stood in the back line of the setup
and inconspicuously performed a reli-
able yet unremarkable accompaniment
to the rhythm section of the band.

December 15, 1969

GOT LIVE IF YOU WANT IT

For his first concert appearance to
a British audience since 1966, John
hastily convened a group of musicians,
including fellow Beatle George, onstage
for a charity evening of music and fun
at London's Lyceum Ballroom. John's
reasoning for the gig was twofold: to
raise a considerable amount of money
for UNICEF and to record the concert
for later release. The Plastic Ono Band,
in all its nebulous glory, performed a
23-minute set combining just two
songs, their latest hit record *Cold
Turkey*, and Yoko's harrowing track,
"Don't Worry Kyoko (Mummy's Only
Looking for Her Hand in the Snow)."

January 16, 1970

SELF-PORTRAITS

John and Yoko had already premiered a film revealing John's penis in various stages of erection, and he would further mine the theme of erotica with an exhibition of self-penned, highly personal lithographs. The 14 pictures, depicting John in various stages of sexual entanglement with Yoko, predictably ignited yet another bout of Lennon bashing in the media, who were by now thoroughly sick and tired of his apparent determination to self-destruct as a Beatle. Although the champagne was flowing on opening night, the bubbly appreciation would be short-lived. Scotland Yard's Obscene Publication Squad would visit the exhibition at the London Arts Gallery the day after the opening and remove a number of pictures for "examination." The gallery would eventually be sued for displaying the pictures, but at a court hearing it would be acquitted of any impropriety in showing them to the public.

Ringo: "John and Yoko? Some people think they're mad, but he's only being John."

February 2, 1970

PLEASED TO MEET YOU
Ringo and wife Maureen at London's
Heathrow returning home after a
working holiday in the States. The
couple had been on the West Coast
principally for a gala premiere
of Ringo's latest film, *The Magic
Christian*, although they did manage
to sneak in a performance by Elvis
Presley, in his new cabaret persona,
during their stay in Las Vegas.

LIVING IN HARMONY

John and Yoko weren't the only ones
doing their bit for world harmony.
George, through the gentle energies of
Krishna consciousness, was spreading
the word of increased vibrations
through meditation and strict obedi-
ence to the word of the Lord. Giving
the fledgling U.K.-based wing of the
Krishna movement a considerable
boost, George recorded a version of
the Hare Krishna mantra with follow-
ers from the London order of the movement. George produced the repetitive
chant, used in daily worship by Krishna
devotees, at Abbey Road studios.
Taking a leaf out of the Beatles' campaign book, George also took the band
of spiritual minstrels onto the roof of
the Apple headquarters in London to
formally launch the single.

March 12, 1970

FRIAR PARK, HENLEY-ON-THAMES

For more than five years George had
lived in a modest bungalow on the
fringes of London's stockbroker belt in
Surrey. The modern look of the Esher
property was a hit with the young
Harrison when he purchased it in
1965, but in 1970 his newly found spir-
ituality demanded something a bit
more in keeping with the world's most
recognizable mystic. Friar Park, a run-
down manor house in the leafy envi-
rons of Henley-on-Thames, was up for
sale, and the Beatle instantly fell in love
with the 80-room property. He ultimately poured hundreds of thousands
of pounds into the manor and its lavish
grounds, restoring them to their
former glory.

OH WOMAN, OH WHY?
The McCartneys put on a show of
unity as they put the final touches on
their debut single, "Another Day," and
its B-side, "Oh Woman, Oh Why?"

SOBER AND DEFIANT

Paul and Linda leaving the rear exit of London's High Court of Justice in the Strand after attending hearings regarding the breakup of the Beatles' partnership. Paul had instigated the proceedings after taking exception to the appointment of Allen Klein as manager and had cited the gradual disintegration of the band in bringing his action.

Klein had long set his sights on the management of the group, and after Epstein's death, made tentative steps to secure them. After talks with John, Ringo, and George in early 1969, he received the patronage of 75 percent of the group. Paul, however, would be the hardest to win over. Having recently married Linda Eastman, Paul had wanted his father-in-law, Lee (an entertainment lawyer), to take over the group's affairs and therein lay the conflict. Feeling that Paul had vested interests in his choice, the other Beatles refused to budge and so Paul was left with no option but to sue his former partners. Paul won his battle, but the whole sorry saga of the Beatles' demise had to be aired in full view of the public.

John: "Paul's criticisms of Allen Klein may reflect his dislike of the man, but I don't think they are fair. Klein is certainly forceful to an extreme but he does get results. He didn't sow discord between us."

Paul: "All summer long in Scotland I was fighting with myself as to whether I should do anything like that. It was murderous. I had a knot in my stomach all summer. . . . My biggest problem was I had to sue the Beatles; I tried to sue Allen Klein, but he wasn't a party to any of the agreements, so I ended up having to sue my best friends as a technical matter. It was the last thing in the world I wanted to do, but it was pointed out to me that it was the only way to do it."

DON'T WORRY, KYOKO

John and a distraught Yoko arrive in
Paris after the drama of an alleged
abduction of Yoko's child, Kyoko, in
Spain. Authorities had detained the
couple for a short period in Majorca
after Yoko's former husband, Anthony
Cox, had claimed to local police that
they had kidnapped the child while in
his care. However, as specified in their
divorce hearing, while Cox had been
granted visitation rights, it was Yoko
who retained full custody of Kyoko.
Nevertheless, Cox refused to give the
child over to the Lennons when they
arrived to collect her and subsequently
went to the police.

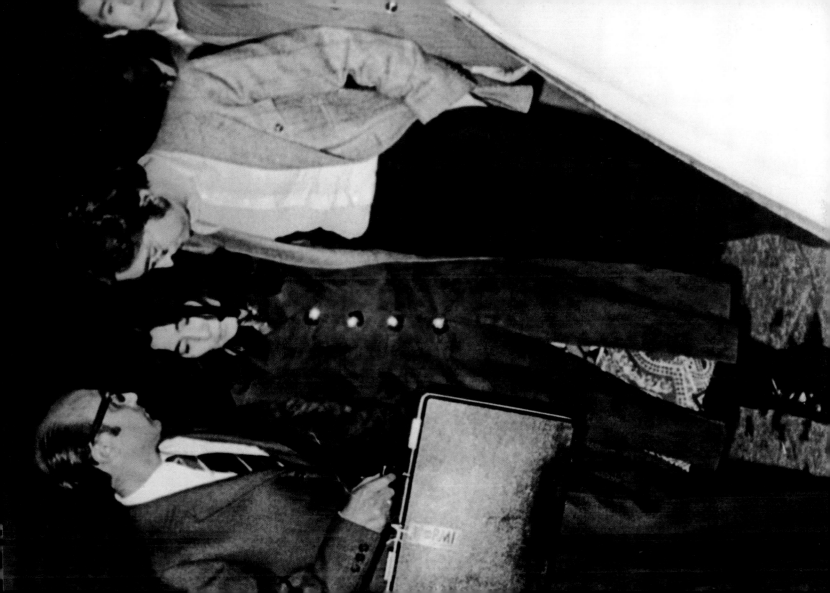

May 12, 1971

A BRIEF RESPITE

Paul and Linda with children Mary
and Heather, en route to Mick Jagger's
wedding in the south of France. The
family flew to fashionable Saint-Tropez
to attend what the press had dubbed
"the wedding of the decade." Still
embroiled in the Beatles' legal affairs,
the "ex-Beatle" (something Paul constantly referred to himself as) had
retreated to his Scottish farm and
had become something of a recluse.

July 14, 1971

John and Yoko return from a trip to
New York that had included a highly
charged appearance onstage with
Frank Zappa and the Mothers of
Invention. The couple's return to
England was timed to coincide with
the reissue of *Grapefruit*, Yoko's conceptual, if at times wholly unfath-
omable, art and verse collection.

John: "A lot of people who read the
book when it was first published . . .
are now professors of American uni-
versities, and *Grapefruit* is part of the
curriculum in film schools."

August 1, 1971

THE CONCERT FOR BANGLADESH
Flanked by Bob Dylan and Leon Russell,
George performs to save a generation at
Madison Square Garden in New York.
Moved by the harrowing scenes relayed
from war-torn Bangladesh, George put
together two benefit shows to raise
much-needed finances to help alleviate
the suffering in the region. With support from sitarist Ravi Shankar, George
was able to coax the finest of the world's
musicians to play an emotional concert,
in hindsight the first benefit concert to
be staged by rock's fraternity.

George: "We had to get this together quickly so I had to put myself
out there and hope for friends to
support me."

December 1980 (this page)   Early 1970s (opposite)

TAKE THESE WINGS...

Of all the Beatles' solo ventures, it was Paul's loose collaboration with Wings that found most favor with the buying public. Paul's talent for crafting unforgettable pop tunes helped Wings dominate the charts on both sides of the Atlantic during the 1970s.

December 1980

THE UNTHINKABLE

Just weeks after this picture was taken,
John was dead, the victim of a crazed
assassin's bullet. John, who had lived
virtually incognito for five years following the birth of his son, Sean, had
been thrust back into the spotlight with
the release of his collaborative album
with Yoko, *Double Fantasy.*

John: "People come up and ask me for
autographs or say 'hi,' but they won't
bug you. Do you wanna know how
good that feels?"

June 1, 1987

Ringo with wife and actress Barbara
Bach at a charity auction in support of
the AIDS Crisis Trust at Christie's in
London. A party fixture during the
1970s and 1980s, the couple would
eventually seek professional help for
their excesses, which eventually led
them to adopt a more conventional
lifestyle.

AIDS CRISIS TRUST

Bibliography

BOOKS

Bedford, Carol. *Waiting for the Beatles: An Apple Scruff's Story*. Dorset, England: Blandford Press, 1984.

Braun, Michael. *Love Me Do: The Beatles Progress*. N.p.: Penguin, 1964.

Brown, Peter, and Steven Gaines. *The Love You Make: An Insider's Story of the Beatles*. New York: McGraw-Hill, 1983.

Carr, Roy, and Tony Tyler. *The Beatles: An Illustrated Record*. London?: New English Library, 1974.

Catterall, Ali, and Simon Wells. *Your Face Here: British Cult Movies Since the 1960s*. New York: Fourth Estate, 2001.

Clayson, Alan. *The Quiet One: A Life of George Harrison*. London: Sidgwick and Jackson, 1990.

————. *Ringo Starr: Straight Man or Joker*. London: Sidgwick and Jackson, 1991.

Coleman, Ray. *John Winston Lennon and John Ono Lennon*. London: Sidgwick and Jackson, 1984.

————. *Brian Epstein: The Man Who Made the Beatles*. New York: Viking, 1989.

Epstein, Brian. *A Cellarful of Noise*. New York: Souvenir Press, 1964.

Flippo, Chet. *McCartney, the Biography*. London: Sidgwick and Jackson, 1988.

Gunther, Curt and A.J.S. Rayl. *Beatles '64: A Hard Day's Night in America*. London: Sidgwick and Jackson, 1989.

Davies, Andy. *The Beatles Files*. London: Bramley Books, 1998.

Lennon, Cynthia. *A Twist of Lennon*. N.p.: Star Books, 1978.

Lennon, John. *Lennon Remembers*. New York: Penguin, 1971.

Lewisohn, Mark. *Here, There and Everywhere: The Beatles Live!* London: Pavilion Books, 1986.

————. *The Beatles' Recording Sessions*. London: Hamlyn, 1988.

————. *The Beatles: 25 Years in the Life, 1962–1987*. London: Sidgwick and Jackson, 1987.

————. *The Complete Beatles Chronicle*. Salem, MA: Pyramind Books, 1992.

Lewisohn, Mark, Piet Schreuders, and Adam Smith. *The Beatles London*. London: Pavilion Books, 1994.

Miles, Barry, ed. *The Beatles in Their Own Words*. Adelaide: Omnibus Books, 1978.

Norman, Philip. *Shout! The True Story of the Beatles*. London: Elm Tree Books, 1981.

Schafner, Nicholas. *The Beatles Forever*. New York: McGraw-Hill, 1977.

Taylor, Derek. *As Time Passes By*. London: Abacus, 1974.

Tremlett, George. *The Paul McCartney Story*. N.p.: Futura, 1975.

MAGAZINES

The Beatles Book Monthly: 1963-2001
Life: Beatles' Reunion Special, Fall 1995
Look Magazine, December 13, 1966
Mojo: Beatles Special, 1000 Days of Beatlemania, 3 issues, 2002–03
Mojo, September 2004
Playboy Magazine, February 1965
Uncut, July 2004

WEB SITES

Beatles Ultimate Experience: http://www.geocities.com/~beatleboy1/db.menu.html

Beatles Transcription Database: http://members.aol.com/dinsdalep/interdex.html

AUDIO SOURCES

"The Mersey Sound," BBC, October 9, 1963
"Follow the Beatles," BBC, August 3, 1964
"Roving Report," ITN, December 20, 1966
ITN News, June 19, 1967
The Beatles Tapes, Polydor, 1977

Acknowledgments

SPECIAL THANKS TO THE FOLLOWING PEOPLE: Charles Merullo, Liz Ihre, Matt Butson, Tea McAleer, Bob Ahearn, and everyone at Getty Images and W9 in London for their support of this project from its inception to completion; Christopher Sweet, Andrea Danese, Robert McKee, Isa Loundon, and the rest at Abrams for putting it all together; the magnificent Paolo Hewitt for support above and beyond the call of duty; Tim, Mike, Phil, and all the other FR crew for love, laughs, and a decent cup of tea; everybody at Orchard Court for welcoming me into their "family" at a difficult time; and Kensington Library for their understanding of my continual lateness.

Mark Lewisohn's unique contribution to Beatles history cannot be overstated. Over the years Lewisohn's research has unearthed a truly remarkable library of information that, as time passes and memories fade, has preserved an exact calendar of a remarkable phenomenon. The Beatles deserve no finer chronicler of their history, and I would like to thank him for his generosity of time and genial spirit.

And finally, an extra special thanks go to Bob, Brooke, and Beatles fans everywhere.

Simon Wells

To my long-suffering father, Phillip, who has tolerated his son's obsession with the Beatles for over forty years.—SW

Acquiring Editor: Christopher Sweet
Editor: Andrea Danese
Designer: Robert McKee
Production Manager: Jane Searle

B+T 29.95 11/05

Library of Congress Cataloging-in-
Publication Data
Wells, Simon, 1961–
  The Beatles : 365 days / by Simon Wells.
    p. cm.
  Includes bibliographical references and
index.
  ISBN 0–8109–5911–9 (hardcover : alk.
paper)
  1. Beatles—Pictorial works. I. Title.
  ML421.B4W45 2005
  782.42166'092'2—dc22
       2005000171

10 9 8 7 6 5 4 3 2 1

ABRAMS

Harry N. Abrams, Inc.
100 Fifth Avenue
New York, N.Y. 10011
www.abramsbooks.com

Abrams is a subsidiary of

LA MARTINIÈRE
GROUPE